PRAISE FOR *GR*

"*Grow* is a *must-read* for anyone aspiring to build the skills, insight, and lessons to reach their full career potential. In addition to very hard work and unwavering focus, mentorship is essential to every high performer and Randy's book is like having a great coach by your side."

—RAFAEL ILISHAYEV, co-founder and co-CEO, Gopuff

"Randy's book *Grow* is an effective and practical guide to advancing your career in any environment. His clear and concise steps drive positive career outcomes and enable people to expand their scope of leadership."

—DAVE PEACOCK, former president, Anheuser-Busch InBev and Schnuck Markets

"Randy Ornstein has cracked the code on what it takes to get promoted in the post-pandemic business world. His book *Grow* provides step-by-step instructions on how to get ahead and is filled with intriguing behind-the-scenes anecdotes and experiences. Grab this easy-to-read book for your next flight and it'll fly by in no time!"

—BRIAN KELLY, founder, The Points Guy

"I read and thoroughly enjoyed Randy's book—his lessons learned are accurate, real-life, and practical. When I recruited him at Indiana University to join my IRI Client Service Team, apparently, I saw more in him than he did in himself. I saw a future Hall of Famer who was very smart, possessed a deep-seated desire to succeed, was a problem solver, an innovative thinker, and a soft-spoken young man who would succeed at anything he put his mind to doing. His book reveals that everything I thought he could do, he did do! I'm proud to call him my friend and continue to expect more great accomplishments from him in the future. His book is a must-read for everyone who has high aspirations of themselves."

—**BUMP WILLIAMS**, president and CEO, Bump Williams Consulting

"I had a front row seat for the majority of the career development and promotions described in *Grow* by Randy Ornstein. I'd recommend this to all professionals entering the world of business."

—**CHRIS WILLIAMS**, executive vice president of National Accounts, Southern Glazer's Wine and Spirits; former SVP, Anheuser-Busch National Retail Sales

"*Grow* is an essential read for anyone looking to elevate their career to new heights. If there's a will there's a way and Randy demonstrates how to effectively climb the career ladder while enjoying the ride. It's a must for those looking to leapfrog the competition and rise to the top!"

—**JOSH WAND**, founder and motivator in chief at ForceBrands, PINATA, and The Family Fund & Founder Community

THE

ESSENTIAL

GUIDE TO

GETTING

PROMOTED

GROW

RANDY ORNSTEIN with Hayley Ornstein

RIVER GROVE
BOOKS

Published by River Grove Books
Austin, TX
www.rivergrovebooks.com

Distributed by River Grove Books

Design and composition by Greenleaf Book Group and Brian Phillips
Cover design by Greenleaf Book Group and Brian Phillips
Cover images ©3DJustincase. Used under license from Shutterstock.com

Publisher's Cataloging-in-Publication data is available.

Print ISBN: 978-1-63299-593-3

eBook ISBN: 978-1-63299-594-0

First Edition

To all my bosses, each of whom taught me
different lessons about how to get promoted:

Sara
Lori
Heather
Denny
Terry
Mark
Clayton
CJ
Mike
Chris
Ari
Alex
Brendan
Pat
George
Chris
Maria

CONTENTS

Foreword by Hayley Ornstein   ix

Preface   xi

Introduction: Promotion Is within Your Reach   1

PART 1: Everyday Excellence   7

   CHAPTER 1: Maximize Meetings   9

   CHAPTER 2: Manage Your Messages   20

   CHAPTER 3: Study for Success   39

   CHAPTER 4: Take Control of Your Day   52

   CHAPTER 5: Help Your Team Succeed   67

PART 2: Going Above and Beyond   91

   CHAPTER 6: Create Best Practices   93

   CHAPTER 7: Solve Problems Systematically   103

   CHAPTER 8: Get the Yes   111

   CHAPTER 9: Present Like a Pro   129

   CHAPTER 10: Invest in Your Future   142

Conclusion   157

Appendix 1   159

Appendix 2   163

Acknowledgments   165

Notes   169

About the Author   179

FOREWORD

IN THE SUMMER OF 2008, Anheuser-Busch (A-B) was acquired by InBev, a Belgium company. Randy was early in his career and had been working at A-B for 3 years. We were living in Arkansas at the time but had family and friends in St. Louis, where television and newspapers continually reported on the merger.

The whole St. Louis community (as well as people around the country) were up in arms about the merger. People boycotted Budweiser. They were angry that a company with a rich family history based in St. Louis was now foreign owned. Internally there were lots of changes in people and budgets. Outside and inside the company, there seemed to be a general sense of negativity about the merger.

When people asked me how it was going for Randy, my response was a little different from what might have been expected. "It's actually working out for us," I replied on multiple occasions.

After all, the rumor was that at the old Anheuser-Busch, it wasn't about what you knew; it was about whom you knew. When Randy began at A-B, he worked alongside persons whose parents, uncles, and grandparents had all worked for A-B. Seniority was a significant component to promotion.

"It's working out for us," I remember saying. "They are now promoting people based on performance rather than seniority. Randy's quickly moving up in the company."

In essence, *Grow* is a story of Randy's promotions. In *Grow*, Randy shares the strategies he used to get promoted at Anheuser-Busch. These are the strategies that allowed him to stand out as an entry-level Category Space Manager and go on to hold multiple VP-level jobs at A-B. These are the strategies he continues to use in his career at Gopuff.

Randy is not keeping these strategies close at hand or sharing them with only a select few within his network. Instead, he aims to reach as many people as possible and help them realize their career potential for financial and personal growth.

I personally hope persons of all backgrounds, education levels, and socioeconomic statuses can benefit from *Grow*. For far too long, promotions within corporations—whether intentionally or unintentionally—have favored those in these privileged positions. They have favored those for whom industry knowledge was discussed at the dinner table and business connections solidified through familial and social networks, which often lacked cultural or socioeconomic diversity.

I hope *Grow* can be a resource for those without access to networks from country clubs and elite educational institutions. I hope *Grow* can help persons who may not have had the extra advantages afforded, currently and historically, to many within executive positions.

I believe that anyone who desires and is motivated to advance their career can benefit from the strategies delivered in this book. I hope that *Grow* can play a small part in leveling the playing field.

Hayley Ornstein

PREFACE

I ROSE UP THE RANKS at one of the largest consumer packaged goods companies in the world, Anheuser-Busch InBev (A-B). I started in an entry-level position and went on to hold four different Vice President positions over five years. Now, I am Senior Director of Beverages at Gopuff, the creator and current leader in the instant needs category. No, I didn't game the system, fudge my resume, or discredit my coworkers. I figured out what excites my management and focused on refining and executing those skills. I figured out how to get my management to think of me when it was time to fill that next position.

For many years at A-B, I was asked to give a speech to new hires after they completed a Sales Development Trainee Program. My commencement ceremony speech always included tips on growing professionally and getting promoted. I started with these five tips and added more each year.

1. Data is power, so know your numbers

2. Work as a team, but don't be overly agreeable

3. Have a sense of urgency in everything you do

4. Go above and beyond and be memorable

5. Be persistent to get what you need

I consistently received positive feedback about my speeches. Employees would even bring up the tips in conversations with me years later. Now, every time I join a new team or add new team members, I go over my ever-expanding list of tips.

I share these tips with my teams because I want them to succeed. When my team does well, I do well. Though my real motivation to help coworkers goes beyond strengthening my individual status, team, or company. I am motivated because I passionately enjoy teaching and mentoring.

One of the most exciting and rewarding parts of my job is when I get to help an employee get promoted. After my first promotion, I became a manager. I was now responsible for evaluating my colleague and was given the criteria with which to do so. For me, this was like being handed the answer key to a test.

Since then, I have felt the need to help the people I manage master the test and get promoted.

I wrote this book so you too can get promoted. In this book I will be sharing tangible strategies that helped me get to where I am today in my career. These are the strategies I share with my team and mentees. These are the strategies that helped me get promoted. And these are the strategies that will help you get promoted

I didn't come up with all these strategies on my own. I've had great bosses, each with their own unique strengths. These bosses have been my teachers and mentors. I've incorporated their advice, as well as recommendations from coworkers and colleagues. I've also looked to experts in business and psychology to refine and provide support for these strategies. As a result, when you read this book, you will be benefiting not only from my insight and experience, but also from the insights and experiences of those who came before me. My hope is that you can adapt this information to your profession, workplace, and job to help yourself, your team, and your company.

In *Grow,* you will find tips and best practices to incorporate into your daily work life to help you stand out and get promoted. These are the techniques that helped me move up the ranks from an entry-level position all the way up to Vice President at one of the largest beverage companies in the world. These are the strategies that worked for me, and I believe these are the strategies that will work for you.

Are you ready to elevate your career to new heights?

PROMOTION IS WITHIN YOUR REACH

I AM NOT A GENIUS who graduated at the top of his class or had an Ivy League education. I struggled with some subjects in school, especially English. I have a hard time paying attention and am also rather quiet. Yet, after entering the workforce, I rose up the ranks at one of the largest consumer packaged goods (CPG) companies in the world, Anheuser-Busch InBev (A-B). I was promoted seven times at A-B, all before the age of forty. From there, I joined Gopuff and helped them grow into a leader within the instant-needs category.

After graduating college with a degree in business, I took a job with Information Resources, Inc. (IRI), a data analytics and market research company. I was on their Anheuser-Busch team and worked in A-B's Chicago office. I remember looking in amazement at the Vice Presidents' offices, with their names on gold plates by the side of their doors. I wondered how they ever got to be in such a high position. I was pretty sure that level of success was beyond my reach. I didn't think I had it in me. I had been an average student at a public college. I thought of myself as an average employee; nothing special.

At that time, I was good at my job, but I wasn't driven to move up the corporate ladder. Nor did I even know how. I left work every day at five p.m., didn't put in extra hours, and never thought about work when I wasn't there. If I had completed all my work by three p.m., I would surf the Internet or play solitaire until it was time for me to leave.

My outlook changed during my first official role at A-B as an entry-level Category Space Manager on A-B's Walmart account. I became skilled in Microsoft Excel and mastered the space-planning software. (Space-planning software allows users to create planograms, virtual pictures of where specific items go on a store's shelves. In our case, these virtual pictures served to communicate where we recommended different beers be placed on Walmart's shelves.) Soon, I was the go-to person if someone had a quick question or needed a report or analysis done ASAP. It didn't take long for my hard work to get noticed by management. After three years as a Category Space Manager, I was promoted to Category Manager. So, instead of just drawing planograms for Walmart, I was now recommending which beers to put on display, which beers to picture in their circulars, and which new beers to add to their shelves.

This promotion was a huge boost to my confidence. I saw the payoffs that came from excelling in my job—and frankly, I was ready for more. I had stopped playing solitaire long ago because I now was too busy constantly trying to improve my work. I no longer saw myself as an average employee with limited career potential. Instead, I began to believe that I was capable of mastering anything my job put in front of me.

It became my mission to continue to move up in the company. I put in the work and quickly rose up the ranks. I was promoted from:

- Category Space Manager to

- Category Manager to

- Senior Category Manager to

- Senior Director of Category Management National Grocery and Drug Chains to

- Vice President of Sales for Walmart and Sam's Club to

- General Manager of Teavana Ready to Drink Iced Tea to

- Vice President of Non-Alcoholic Beverages to

- Vice President of Beyond Beer.

I was promoted again and again and again. Along the way, I learned valuable lessons about what it takes to get ahead and put those lessons in this book.

There are a lot of books and materials out there about how to ask for a raise. This is not that book. I made more money through promotions than would have ever been possible through annual raises. If you are driven to make more money, I say this: rather than focus on convincing someone you deserve a raise, demonstrate through your daily performance in your current role that you are capable of even more. Demonstrate you are worthy of a promotion.

Grow is a book about how to become a better employee. It will teach you how to become the type of employee managers seek out to fill open roles and who is highly recommended by their boss when they apply for a new position. By following the guidance and doing the work recommended in *Grow*, you will build skills, develop habits, and create relationships that will make you a stronger employee now and in the future. If your dream is to climb to the top of a corporation or you have found yourself stagnant in your current role and are ready for advancement, this book is for you.

Part 1 of *Grow* is called Everyday Excellence. Whatever your position, you likely answer emails, attend meetings, and communicate with a team. You may consider these to be mundane, inconsequential tasks that don't significantly influence your career trajectory, but that's incorrect. These everyday tasks provide opportunities to improve productivity and job performance and to change how you're perceived by your boss and colleagues. By excelling in your daily responsibilities, you can stand out and show you have what it takes to be promoted.

- Chapter 1—Maximize Meetings—provides guidance on using meetings to your advantage to show you are an exceptional employee. It includes key tips on maintaining punctuality, paying attention, and speaking up during meetings.

- Chapter 2—Manage Your Messages—helps you sift through what actually matters when it comes to emails and messages. It discusses the importance of responding quickly, staying organized, using headings and bullet points, avoiding unnecessary messages, double-checking your work, and following up.

- Chapter 3—Study for Success—identifies the stuff so important that you should study it and know it like the back of your hand. These essentials include data analytics software as well as statistics and information about you, your projects, and your performance.

- Chapter 4—Take Control of Your Day—talks about taking charge of what happens during your day and when it happens. It goes over the importance of initiating productive meetings and scheduling tasks according to when you will complete them best. It also offers guidance on keeping up with work when traveling for business.

- Chapter 5—Help Your Team Succeed—stresses the importance of working well within a team to help your team succeed. These strategies include using "we" instead of "I," being positive, speaking up, asking for help, acknowledging and taking responsibility for mistakes, and being a team leader.

Part 2, Going Above and Beyond, identifies how to stop performing *only* your day-to-day duties and demonstrate that you want to and can do more. This section provides guidance on how to answer questions, discover problems, and identify solutions to help your customer, team, and company.

- Chapter 6—Create Best Practices—explains how to develop new projects and processes. It identifies and walks you through the essential components of creating a best practice, including finding a problem, receiving feedback, securing support, and ensuring implementation.

- Chapter 7—Solve Problems Systematically—provides a methodical approach to finding answers to questions and solutions to problems. Whether your boss asks you to look into an issue or you're spearheading a new best practice, move forward using a deliberate system that involves clarifying the question, locating relevant data, and presenting your findings.

- Chapter 8—Get the Yes—guides you on how to close the deal through making the ask, using data to persuade, knowing their business, creating an action plan, being trustworthy, and creating a personal connection. Whether it's getting others to agree to your proposal, implementing a new process, or selling your product, you need to Get the Yes!

- Chapter 9—Present Like a Pro—provides tips on how to create a great presentation and clearly communicate information in a way that respects, engages, and prioritizes your audience.

- Chapter 10—Invest in Your Future—identifies what you can do today to succeed in the future. Increase the likelihood that opportunities will come your way by finding a mentor, building friendships, relocating, and switching roles within or between companies.

Whether you work remotely or in an office, whether you are fresh out of college or a veteran employee, *Grow* gives you the information you need to move up in your company.

I cracked the code on how to get promoted. Now, I am sharing what I know with you.

PART 1

EVERYDAY EXCELLENCE

DURING MY CLIMB up the corporate ladder, it became clear that promotions had a lot to do with a person's ability to perform day-to-day tasks especially well. As an A-B Category Space Manager, for example, I didn't need to be an expert writer or up on current events. I didn't even need to know the ins and outs of how beer was made. What I did need to know was how to quickly and flawlessly create planograms[*1] for every Walmart store that carried beer. In other words, I needed to know how to do my job.

To be fair, my job entailed more than creating planograms. I needed to communicate with wholesalers, Beer Buyers, and retail managers clearly and promptly. I needed to be able to analyze data, work collaboratively with my team, and sometimes get a lot of work done within a short period. So, these were the areas I prioritized. I didn't need to know statistics about wine or liquor consumption (at that time). I needed to know stats about beer sales, and those were the stats that I studied. In other words, I homed in on the most important, most pertinent information that affected my everyday performance.

Planograms are detailed drawings, used by most retailers, to delineate where to put products on a shelf to maximize sales. Planograms take into account shelf space and visual merchandising strategies.

Part 1 of *Grow* focuses on fine-tuning those fundamental areas that influence everyday performance. Before doing the extras (see Part 2, Going Above and Beyond), focus on the basics and learn to execute your daily responsibilities exceptionally well. These basic, yet essential, day-to-day responsibilities include staying on top of emails, getting along with your coworkers, and being prepared for meetings.

Research has found that job performance (i.e., getting along with others, completing tasks on time, achieving work goals) is the factor most associated with career mobility and promotion prospects.[2] Employees who perform their job well are more likely to get promoted. So, stand out as someone who is ready to be promoted by executing your fundamental job responsibilities flawlessly. Display everyday excellence.

CHAPTER 1

MAXIMIZE MEETINGS

ON FRIDAY, MARCH 13, 2020, community transmission of the coronavirus was confirmed within the Philadelphia area. The instant-needs delivery company Gopuff instructed its corporate employees to start working from home the following Monday. During this time, the term "meeting" broadened for me and millions of others around the country who began working remotely. Communication that used to happen informally at the office now took place during virtual meetings via computer screen. Many telephone calls also became virtual meetings. And then there were the regular meetings that were still on but now virtual. Back-to-back virtual meetings now filled my daily schedule.

Virtual meetings have now become integrated and commonplace in business communication. Still, in-person meetings are far from extinct. This means employees are expected to know how to participate in both virtual and in-person meetings. Whether on a computer or in a boardroom, you must know how to put your best foot forward during a meeting.

In this chapter, Maximize Meetings, I will share important tips on attending meetings virtually and in person. I will review etiquette and give advice about speaking up, attentiveness, and punctuality. I will teach you how to not just make it through a meeting but how to use meetings to your advantage to show you have what it takes to be promoted.

SPEAK UP

I want people on my team to speak up during meetings. Meetings are rarely intended to be one-way conversations. Instead, most meetings are two-way dialogues where the organizer asks for questions, clarification, or feedback. If you're in a meeting with five people or fewer, you are expected to speak up. You were added to that meeting for a reason. If you're in a meeting and don't contribute anything, why are you even there? If the meeting organizer thought you were not needed, they would not have included you. When I present, I want feedback from all attendees, regardless of their role, title, or level of seniority.

I once had two entry-level employees on my team who rarely spoke up at meetings. I found this disappointing because, in many meetings, I was particularly interested in their opinions, as they were the only females on the team. When I mentioned to them in one-on-one discussions that I would like them to speak up more during meetings, they each shared that they felt it was not their place to speak up when surrounded by more senior coworkers. I told them that I valued everyone's input, regardless of their title. I explained that our team is stronger when we hear diverse perspectives, and if only my two senior people are speaking up, then we're not getting that diversity of thought.

Ideas, projects, and teams become more innovative and stronger when different perspectives are heard. Each employee has a unique point of view, given their age, gender, culture, and experiences. Junior employees often provide some of the best insights and ideas because they offer a fresh, outside set of eyes that more senior members can't offer. If you're a junior employee who is not speaking up at meetings, you're limiting how much you are helping your team (and your future career).

If you want to speak up but are unsure what to say, consider asking a question. Questions are great because they show intellectual humility. You're acknowledging that you don't have all the answers, but other people in the room might. Questions can also spur discussion. Renowned author Daniel Pink notes that "questions are inherently interactive [in that] they invoke a response" from others.[1] Remember, no one expects you to have all the answers, but you are expected to help others think more deeply about the issues. Questions are a great way to do that.

Your contribution does not need to be profound or groundbreaking. If a meeting is informational, you could compliment the presenter and share how you plan to use the information. If the presenter is asking for feedback about an idea, at a minimum, speak up and let the group know that you are in agreement.* In most cases, contributing something is better than saying nothing.

In addition to speaking up at meetings, it is also important to be an active audience member during presentations. Questions and comments provide the presenter with feedback that their message was heard and made sense. Questions also allow the presenter to share additional information and provide clarification. Believe it or not, most presenters sincerely want to hear from their

---

*If you are able, state your ideas right there in the meeting, instead of a day or two later during a private meeting. Your message will be more impactful if you chime in while the topic is still fresh in everyone's mind; it also shows that you are quick on your feet and not afraid to speak up in a group. Your coworkers will soon learn to be on their toes when they present.

audience. When no one has anything to say, a presenter can't help but wonder if anyone was even listening.

At the end of a presentation, presenters traditionally ask if there are any questions, and this is almost always followed by a lull. I recommend you take advantage of this moment of silence to speak up. While being the first person to speak up can be intimidating, it is usually easier than trying to interject or talk over others once comments start. Once a discussion gets rolling, two people inevitably end up talking at the same time, and one person has to back down. The person who backs down may never get another chance to speak. Instead of fighting to get a word in, be the first one to speak up. You'll stand out and help pave the way for productive discussion.

I remember a time when I was in a large virtual meeting. The presentation ended and the presenter asked for questions. There were five seconds of complete silence. To me, those five seconds felt like an eternity. I felt bad for the presenter. I could see the disappointment in her eyes when there weren't any questions, and I was in complete disbelief that no one in this sixty-person meeting had the courage to speak up.

I quickly came up with a question when I saw she was about to call the meeting to an end. I don't think my question was particularly insightful, but it broke the ice and led to five other people speaking up. The discussion ended up providing valuable insights to the group. If I had not asked that initial ice-breaking question, the meeting would have ended. Interestingly, when this presenter led another meeting two weeks later, the same thing happened when she asked for questions. No one spoke up. But this time, after a few seconds of silence, instead of closing the meeting, the presenter said, "Randy, what do you have for us?" When you speak up, you stand out, encourage productive conversation, and possibly save the day for the presenter.

Don't assume that you will come up with something (of value) to say on the fly, particularly when put on-the-spot. Accordingly, I recommend taking notes and jotting down questions during meetings. This will help when it's time for discussion or if you're asked directly for your thoughts. I also recommend preparing for meetings. Give yourself an edge by doing your homework and arriving at meetings ready to contribute.

Preparing for a meeting can be as straightforward as reviewing key points: what the meeting is about, the agenda, and who will be attending. If there was information (a preread) sent out beforehand, read it. Think ahead of time about what questions will be asked of the group and, more importantly, what questions may be directed specifically toward you. Come prepared to answer those questions. (I'll discuss this more in Chapter 3, Study for Success.)

For example, every Monday I go over weekly Gopuff beverage sales with my team. We look for changes in the data, and I ask the group to offer explanations for anomalies. If you were on my team and leading the wine category, I recommend you go over the wine sales ahead of time. Before the meeting, look for anomalies yourself and research potential explanations. Anticipating questions enables you to provide more accurate and valuable information within a meeting.

You will be more likely to be included in discussions when you seem engaged. Maintain eye contact and don't multitask. If you are in a virtual meeting, turn on your camera, even if other attendees aren't. This conveys that you are invested in and planning to be involved in the meeting. As a rule of thumb (unless it's an extenuating circumstance), don't be camera shy.

Speaking up during virtual meetings can sometimes be tricky. You may need to put extra effort into making your voice heard, particularly when a presenter cannot see part or all of their audience. If you're having difficulty getting called on (and the presenter isn't pausing for questions) raise your virtual hand. If this doesn't work, try unmuting yourself. The speaker may notice and get the signal that you have something to say. If the presenter still doesn't notice you, write the question in the chat box. Asking questions in the chat is commonplace during virtual meetings with a large number of attendees. If none of these tips are working, you'll have to be aggressive and work your way in when there's a pause.

During in-person meetings, speakers are usually able to scan the room and stop if someone raises their hand or looks confused. However, if you're raising your hand during an in-person meeting and the speaker doesn't notice you, it is okay to call out "I have a question" or "I have a comment" when the speaker pauses.

In large meetings, such as those with twenty or more people, the best time to speak up is when the presenter pauses and asks for questions. If the meeting is running short on time or too much is going on for you to say something, send a note to the speaker or applicable parties after the meeting. Especially if you think your comment is valuable.

When speaking up during virtual meetings, mistakes are going to happen. They happen to me, they happen to CEOs, and they will happen to you. And although they're inevitable, they can still cause you to feel discombobulated. Here are some personal examples:

- The Internet was slow, and people couldn't hear me.
- I tried to mute myself and left the meeting accidentally.

◆ I started talking at the same time as someone else. We paused and then started talking again simultaneously (multiple times in a row).

When mistakes like this happen, I recommend you do not waste meeting time going on (and on) about what happened. No need to apologize, joke about, or provide explanations for the mistake. Simply maintain your composure and get back to business.

For example, if (or when) you forget to unmute yourself when speaking, there's no need to say, "Sorry, I was on mute." Just say what you want to say and move on with the meeting. The error of forgetting to unmute yourself happens in almost every one of my virtual meetings. Someone starts talking, but no one can hear them because they're still muted. When it happens, try not to get flustered. Don't let a technical error take away your mojo and keep you from speaking up and contributing.

Don't remain silent during meetings. Meetings are a time for discussion and critical thinking. You are there to listen, learn, and contribute. Don't undervalue the contribution you can make with a question or comment. Do what you can to speak up and ensure you and your ideas are heard. Speaking up demonstrates that you have something to contribute to your team and your company. When I look for people to promote, I choose people who speak up in meetings.

PAY ATTENTION

One of the most important things you can do in a meeting is pay attention. I have been guilty of not paying attention during many meetings. It's easy to get distracted. There have been times when I wasn't listening, was asked a question, and had to ask for the question to be repeated. (FYI, asking someone to repeat themselves is usually a dead giveaway that you weren't paying attention.)

Paying attention during virtual meetings can be particularly challenging. Everything on your computer is accessible. Emails and Slack messages pop up, and there are endless temptations to multitask. While you can typically get away with attending to a few extraneous items during a virtual meeting, the key is to not do this during important meetings.

If you're not sure whether a meeting falls into the category of "important," here are some guidelines. Important meetings include one-on-one meetings, small meetings with your boss, meetings where you are presenting for all or a portion of the time, meetings in which you can add value, and meetings that offer you the opportunity to give your opinion or feedback.

If you think you can listen and work during a virtual non-important meeting, do so discreetly. However, you may not be as sneaky as you think. If your eyes are moving left to right, people can see you're reading. If you're not on mute, people can hear you typing. You get the picture. So, proceed with caution. However, if you really want to attend a meeting like a pro, don't attempt to work on other things simultaneously.

It's standard practice in many top companies for employees to refrain from multitasking and focus exclusively on the meeting. As the General Manager of Teavana Ready to Drink Iced Tea, I attended meetings at the Starbucks headquarters in Seattle. There, I noticed that part of their company culture includes everyone putting away their phones and computers to focus on the meeting. (These were in-person meetings.) I was amazed by the level of decorum, commitment, and productivity this brought to the meetings.

Still, within some companies, it is commonplace for people to multitask during meetings. However, it's not going to be a successful meeting if everyone's multitasking. If your company's culture doesn't include the expectation that workers will give 100% of their attention, you can use that to your advantage. Stand out from your coworkers by giving your full attention and showing the utmost respect to presenters during meetings.

One way to help you pay attention during meetings is by taking notes. You can take notes in a notebook or on your laptop. However, if I will be using my laptop for notetaking during an in-person meeting, I often tell the presenter this at the beginning of the meeting, since it can be distracting for a presenter to see people looking at their laptops instead of at the presentation. If you do type during a meeting, try to type softly. Loud, aggressive typing can be annoying.

You cannot contribute to a meeting if you are not paying attention or are working on other things. When you pay attention during meetings, you can take advantage of opportunities to add value and showcase your talents. Show your boss and coworkers that you are there to contribute by paying attention during meetings.

BE ON TIME

Punctuality is important. Being late for a meeting is not a good look. In fact, lateness negatively correlates with career mobility.[2]

You don't want to be the person whose name is called out by the presenter, "Where is Lauren?" or "Where is David?" (followed by silence). Similarly, you don't want to be that person who shows up five minutes late to a meeting and struggles to find the only open seat at the front of a room packed with hundreds of people while the most senior presenter watches you. These are the situations people don't forget, and that can impact your career.

It is nearly impossible to be on time every single time. You could be in another meeting that runs over; your Internet could be giving you problems; or you could be stuck in traffic. There are always going to be things outside of your control. Therefore, when possible, try to give yourself extra time in case you run into unexpected challenges.

When in person, I typically advise arriving ten minutes early to important meetings. That means you should be parked and at the building at least ten minutes before start time. If you are running late to an in-person meeting to which you are integral, message the meeting organizer that you are running late and potentially ask to call in or attend virtually so you don't miss anything.

With virtual meetings, arriving early is unnecessary and poor etiquette. I recommend joining virtual meetings exactly on time. So, for a 10:30 a.m. meeting, I click connect at 10:30 a.m. For really important virtual meetings, I recommend joining one minute earlier than when the meeting starts. If I am going to be more than two minutes late to a virtual meeting, I let the meeting organizer know about five minutes before start time.

Maintaining punctuality means sometimes having to leave meetings early. You may be in back-to-back meetings and need a restroom break, or you may have overlapping meetings. Most of the time, people understand.

If you know you're going to have to leave a meeting early, try to let the meeting organizer or presenter know ahead of time. If you weren't able to do that and it's a small meeting, just speak up at the beginning of the meeting. Letting the organizer know that you will be leaving early is particularly important if you are scheduled to speak or present, as it allows them an opportunity to rearrange the agenda if necessary.

When it's time for you to leave, speak up and say you need to go or write it in the chat. In larger in-person meetings, try to make eye contact with the meeting organizer while you're leaving and mouth, "I have to go." If it's a 500-person meeting (in-person or virtual), just leave; most likely, no one will miss you.

Being punctual is crucial for making a great impression. Don't be late to meetings. Give the presenter a heads-up if you will be arriving late or dropping off early. By showing up on time, every time, you show that you respect others' time and are ready to contribute.

RECAP

- Make your time during a meeting count. The most important things you can do are pay attention and try to find opportunities to speak up. Remaining silent will not leave a positive impression.

- While you do want to refrain from making huge missteps during a meeting, it's not the end of the world if something goes wrong—especially when relying on technology. If or when you make a mistake, try not to get flustered. Don't take up more meeting time with explanations or apologies. Rather, remedy the situation and move forward.

- Show that you are an employee who adds value to meetings and your company by being on time, listening, asking questions, and providing feedback during meetings.

CHAPTER 2

MANAGE YOUR MESSAGES

WE ALL GET A LOT OF MESSAGES. Some messages are directed to you. Some are directed to you and your team. Some are CCs to keep you in the loop. Some are sent to your whole department or company. And some are SPAM. It's a lot to juggle. However, when you show that you can successfully handle your messages, you show that you can successfully manage your career.

In this chapter, I provide you with strategies to help manage your messages. I go over how to respond quickly to incoming messages and compose clear messages that bring about action. I also provide recommendations on organizing your messages so you can follow up and find old messages quickly. Messages are an extension of who you are, your ideas, and your potential. Use messages to your advantage to help you get promoted.

RESPOND QUICKLY

I have worked with people who take a week to respond to my emails, who never respond, or who respond only after I follow up with them multiple times. It is very frustrating when I feel I am the only one motivated in the interaction. If I feel this way when I don't get a timely response, other people do too.

Given all the tardiness out there, it's clear you will stand out in a positive way when you provide a quick response. A quick reply shouldn't just be for your boss and external customers. It is also important to respond quickly to those you manage. Sociologist Duncan Watts found email response time to be the strongest predictor of employees' satisfaction with their boss. The more time it took for a boss to respond, the more dissatisfied an employee was with their boss.[1] So, when deciding whether to craft "the perfect response" or an "okay," accurate response that you can quickly send, err on the side of being timely. Responding quickly to emails is one of the most impactful and impressive things you can do when communicating with colleagues and customers.

When I was moving up the ladder at A-B, I prided myself on responding quickly to emails. I commonly answered emails within minutes (sometimes within seconds). The recipients were sometimes so impressed with the quick turnaround time that they often sent another email with "Thank you for the quick response." When I was a Category Manager for A-B's Walmart team, Walmart's Beer Buyer told my supervisor, "I enjoy working with Randy because he always shows a sense of urgency. When I send him an email or ask him to do something, regardless of its importance, he gets it done quickly."

Responding to every email, Slack, and text within seconds is unrealistic and unnecessary. All messages don't need to be treated equally. Accordingly, it is important to identify which emails need to take precedence. Messages that hold the highest priority for me are Slacks (or any instant messages) from my boss or an executive officer. I try hard to stop everything and answer these messages immediately.

Other messages to which I try to respond right away, or at most within the hour, include messages that

- use the phrase "please respond ASAP";
- are from my boss, senior management, or a customer;
- are about something that needs correcting right away; or
- are from someone I'm trying to impress.

Unless a later date is identified, I make it a priority to respond to all other messages within twenty-four hours. This twenty-four-hour rule of thumb evolved during my days working with corporate Walmart employees. They followed the Sundown Rule. Supposedly implemented by Sam Walton, who was inspired by the adage "Why put off until tomorrow what you can do today?," the rule stipulated that all emails should be responded to by the end of the day.[2]

Ironically, we often put off answering the most important messages. If it's so important, then why do we procrastinate? Maybe the message contains a question to which we don't know the answer. Maybe it's about a project that's taking longer than expected to complete. Maybe we're not in the right frame of mind to compose a response to a difficult or complex question. Or maybe (this is a frequent one) the issue or sender made you upset and you would rather not deal with it! Still, no matter how tempting, don't procrastinate in responding to important messages!

If you know the email is urgent, instead of putting off replying, send a note to the recipient within the hour telling them you received the message and are working on a response. If the message concerns an incomplete project, inform the sender that you are working on it and plan to have it completed in however many days you need. It is better to manage expectations than to keep someone in the dark about a) whether you received the email and b) the status of their request. As with many things, it's all about managing expectations.

When I was a Category Manager at A-B, my boss cautioned that if a Buyer sends an email with a question or project proposal that is not met with a quick response (or met with an out-of-office reply), they will likely send a note to your competitor. You do not want to lose business to a competitor because you did not respond quickly to an email.

In summary, respond to the most important messages within an hour and most other messages within twenty-four hours. Don't procrastinate replying to messages. If you are unable to properly respond within a day, let the sender know that you received their message and estimate when you will be able to provide them with the necessary information. When you provide quick responses, you communicate that you are respectful, responsive, and on top of your game.

AVOID A MESSY INBOX

If you have hundreds or thousands of emails in your inbox, you likely have a messy inbox. One huge problem with a cluttered inbox is that it's difficult to locate important messages when you need them. For example, imagine being asked about a topic for which you know you have the information, but then you find yourself spending five minutes sifting through your messages to locate it.

When you have a messy inbox, you're also more likely to overlook important messages, and when you do notice them, it may be too late. This example happens to my team at least a few times a year:

A group email containing a question is sent to my team and me. I quickly reply all and respond. Sometime after sending my reply, a team member asks me how they should reply to the message. I tell them, "I replied to it over ten minutes ago." And they say, "Oh, I didn't notice."

To be on top of your game, you need to be aware of every email that enters your inbox. Accordingly, this section offers advice on how to keep a clean, organized inbox so you can spend your time answering questions instead of finding them.

One of the main ways I keep myself organized is by keeping as few emails as possible in my inbox. I used to never leave the office unless I had twenty emails or fewer in my inbox. I admit that having a fixed number can be a bit rigid. While you don't need to have a "maximum occupancy" for your inbox, I do recommend limiting the number of messages that live there.

The only emails remaining in my inbox are "active" messages. These are emails on my "to-do list." I might still need to send a reply or be waiting for someone else to reply (and need to follow up if they don't respond). An email left in my inbox could also serve as a reminder about an active or ongoing project.

After attending to an email, I move it to the appropriate folder within my email server. I created numerous folders to help organize my messages. These include:

- a folder for emails from my boss;

- folders for each one of my direct reports;

- folders for different departments within the company (i.e., finance, HR, legal, marketing);

- folders for current projects;

- a folder for receipts for reimbursement;

- a folder for travel itineraries;

- folders for major accounts (e.g., vendors, suppliers, customers);

- a folder for personal communication; and

- a folder for industry news.

One of my former Walmart Buyers told me that she has an "Action" folder and a "Waiting on Response" folder. Feel free to get creative and find a folder system that works for you.

Get to know your messaging system's settings and use them to your advantage. For example, Gmail allows you to create separate inboxes to separate messages from various senders. In Microsoft Outlook, you can color-code your emails (e.g., red for "urgent," yellow for "be sure to follow up"). Even in Slack, which doesn't offer as many options, you can "star" important contacts, so their messages are always on top. Different messaging systems offer various features to help keep your inbox organized.

In addition to keeping emails organized, save important emails by downloading them onto your computer. Just because an email is put into a folder doesn't mean it is "saved." Some companies' servers delete unsaved emails after only sixty days. For some companies, it's one year. Others may never delete employee emails. Different companies have different policies regarding email retention. So, it is critical to clarify with your company if or when messages may be automatically deleted.

To make sure your emails don't get accidentally deleted, save important emails to an external location, such as a cloud, external drive, or desktop. (Make sure your method for saving is within company policy.) These are examples of emails I generally save:

- An email that serves as a written contract from a retailer or business associate.

- An email from HR that includes financial or health care information.

- An email from someone recognizing your strong efforts (for your annual performance review).

- An email documenting an employee's poor performance (for someone else's annual performance review).

A messy inbox can lead to oversights, frustrations, and wasted time. Create a system for managing and organizing messages. One of the best ways to do this is by limiting the number of messages in your inbox. Put as many emails as possible into folders, save important emails, and delete ones you no longer need. When your inbox is clean and organized, you will be able to locate important information within seconds and be less likely to overlook emails that you don't know are important until it's too late.

USE THE HEADINGS INFORM, FOLLOW-UP, OR ACTION*

I recommend using INFORM, ACTION, or FOLLOW-UP as the first word in the subject line of an email or as the first word

---

*I got this idea from Brian Sedra, a previous direct report of mine. Brian got the idea from one of his former executive leaders. His executive leader wrote "INFORM" on the headline of certain emails that he wanted his team to review more closely. Brian expanded upon this practice by adding the headlines "FOLLOW-UP" and "ACTION." Whenever Brian used one of these three headlines in an email, I took note of the email and knew my role before ever having read the full message.

in a message. This all-caps heading signals to the reader whether the message is to INFORM, bring about ACTION, or provide a FOLLOW-UP. By clearly stating the message's purpose, you stand out as a master communicator and help your recipients stay on top of their messages.

The heading INFORM can be used when a message is intended to provide information. An INFORM message does not require the reader to perform a specific action. The content of an INFORM message could be an industry article, an upcoming program, or an organizational change. I have also used INFORM when sending a group message to management praising an employee's or team's actions.

The ACTION heading signifies that a message includes one or more specific actions for the reader. For example, I have used ACTION when assigning project tasks, asking a question that needs a response, and requesting that a team member contact a client. I recommend saving ACTION for the highest-priority messages. If you overuse ACTION, it will not stand out when you really need it to.

The FOLLOW-UP heading is typically used when the content refers to something previously discussed in a meeting or phone call. For example, I have used FOLLOW-UP when submitting an assignment that had been requested. Typically, FOLLOW-UP messages would include a phrase like "per our discussion."

You do not need to limit yourself to the headings INFORM, ACTION, and FOLLOW-UP. Feel free to get creative and choose headings that fit your specific job. Of course, don't feel the need to use an all-caps header with every message—for example, when replying to someone else's message. Rather, use it at your discretion to help you and your message get noticed.

Now that you've added an eye-catching headline, it's time to create an easy-to-read message. You can do this with bullet points.

BULLET POINT LONG MESSAGES

Long messages can be difficult to read. I often find myself skimming messages after just a few lines and sometimes unintentionally miss important parts. If you don't want to risk your most important information getting lost in a sea of words, try using bullet points when you're writing a long message.

Bullet points can make messages easier to read by breaking up longer paragraphs into shorter, more digestible sentences and guiding the reader to the most essential information. When creating bullet-pointed messages, I recommend the following format:

- A one- to two-sentence introduction.

- Your bullet-pointed sentences.

- A one- to two-sentence summary.

I have found it especially helpful to use bullet points when writing messages that

- recap a meeting or project;

- initiate a project with assigned tasks; or

- include a list.

Consider these two examples:*

EXAMPLE A:

Samantha – It was great meeting you yesterday. We have been working on the follow-ups from our meeting. Please provide me with the upcoming details on the next reset. We have attached a new item form for our new SKUs.*[3] We discussed the feasibility of adding a Teavana six-pack can to our lineup. We are currently working with my supply team and will provide an answer to you by next Thursday on the feasibility of this. If you are interested in a display rack in all of your stores, we need to know by May 1st, so we have time to produce by July. Per your request, we will work with your digital team to add one-dollar-off coupons through your app. My goal is to have everything finalized by next Friday. Let me know if you have any questions.

---

*A stock-keeping unit (SKU) is the scannable bar code printed on product packaging. This label allows vendors to easily look up product information and prices and track inventory.

However, in everyday communication within my industry, the term SKU refers to a specific item being sold. For example, if a beverage brand has six different flavors being sold, we would say "the brand has six SKUs." However, if the brand also offers a variety pack, with the six different flavors in it, the brand would technically have seven SKUs because the variety pack would be its own SKU.

EXAMPLE B:

Samantha – It was great meeting you yesterday. We have been working on the follow-ups from our meeting:

- Please provide me with the upcoming details on the next reset.

- We have attached a new item form for our new SKUs.

- We discussed the feasibility of adding a Teavana six-pack can to our lineup. We are currently working with my supply team and will provide an answer to you by next Thursday on the feasibility of this.

- If you are interested in a display rack in all of your stores, we need to know by May 1st, so we have time to produce by July.

- Per your request, we will work with your digital team to add one-dollar-off coupons through your app.

My goal is to have everything finalized by next Friday. Let me know if you have any questions.

I think it's a no-brainer. The message with bullet points is much easier to read.

When I pull the questions I want answered out of a paragraph and preface them with bullet points, I am more likely to get all my questions answered. In contrast, when my questions are embedded within a long paragraph-form message, the recipients rarely answer all my questions. I typically have to follow up on at least one missed question.

Not only are my bullet-pointed questions more likely to receive responses, but when I send an email with bullet points, the recipient typically writes their response within the text with a different font. Here is an example of how Samantha may have responded to my bullet-pointed email:

Samantha – It was great meeting you yesterday.

We have been working on the follow-ups from our meeting:

- Please provide me with the upcoming details on the next reset. The next reset occurs in mid-June. *My team will provide the assortment decisions by May 1st.*

- We have attached a new item form for our new SKUs. *I have received.*

- We discussed the feasibility of adding a Teavana six-pack can to our lineup. We are currently working with my supply team and will provide an answer to you by next Thursday on the feasibility of this. *Keep me posted.*

- If you are interested in a display rack in all of your stores, we need to know by May 1st, so we have time to produce by July. *Yes, let's make this happen. One rack per store.*

- Per your request, we will work with your digital team to add one-dollar-off coupons through your app. *Let me know when complete.*

When Samantha writes her responses within the text, she does not have to worry about identifying the question she is answering. All she needs to do is type her response. This saves Samantha time and energy.

Using bullet points is a simple way to compose concise, easy-to-read emails that help you and your reader. You don't need to bullet point every email but do consider using bullet points when composing long emails with lots of information. When you make long emails easier to read, you present yourself as an efficient and effective communicator.

DON'T SEND WASTED EMAILS

We all get a lot of emails. As you move up the ranks in your company, your inbox tends to balloon. When emailing customers and coworkers (particularly those in higher positions), be mindful of bombarding them with unnecessary messages. Since your recipient likely gets plenty of emails, send them only those that matter.

On a given day, I must get at least five emails with just the word "thanks" or "thank you." This is an example of what I call a "wasted email." The worst is when multiple people get copied on the one-word reply. This not only creates one wasted email but a wasted email for each of the recipients. Wasted emails are a pet peeve of mine, and I wish everyone would just stop sending unnecessary one-word replies.

Whenever wasted emails become a problem among my teams, I bring it up at a team meeting. I get some laughs, and I can tell a few take offense, but I see the results later in my inbox. I am sure I get made fun of behind my back, but the wasted-email advice isn't just for my benefit. It is for all the other people who receive them—especially our senior management and external contacts. So, I let my team get upset at me instead of having our boss or retailers get upset with them.

I know this is not just a weird personal preference. Once, a Walgreens Buyer emailed me a list of guidelines for communicating with her and her team. One line read "Please don't send 'thank you' emails, the thanks is assumed, and one less email is great."

I likewise emphasize to my team that if you send me an email and I don't respond, it means you provided all the necessary information. If I do respond, it most likely means that I need to follow up about something or want more information. Remember that sometimes no response is a great response.

I'm not a complete Grinch and recognize that showing and receiving appreciation, such as by thanking someone, is a nice thing to do. When I want to provide a quick "thanks," I typically instant message (IM) that person versus expressing my gratitude in an email. Another way to say thank you is by turning a wasted email into a valuable one by elaborating on your thoughts. For example, instead of just writing "thanks," write, "thank you for the information. I appreciate your sense of urgency in providing the data and look forward to an update in two weeks." This small addition turned a wasted email into a valuable one by providing the recipient with specific feedback about which behaviors you most appreciated and a reminder about the date of your next communication.

In addition to the "thank you" email, plenty of other wasted emails can potentially be omitted or expanded upon to add value. Here are some examples of wasted emails and things to consider when deciding whether to omit or expand upon the message:

Scenario	Wasted Email	Things to Consider
Responding to an email that requests your approval	"Aligned"	If you are the fifth person in an email string to write "aligned," can you just reply to the sender vs. replying to all? What other info can you provide on why you approve or do not approve?

Wanting to recognize the sender's great work	"Great recap, Katie!"	Why is the recap great? How can you provide specific feedback about what behaviors are most appreciated? Can you reply just to sender vs. reply to all?
Responding to a request that will be completed within an hour	"I am working on this now and will send over."	If the request will be completed in under an hour, just complete the request and send it instead of sending two emails.

Another often wasteful email is the out-of-office email (which you may be seeing less of in our always-connected, never-in-the-office-anyway, post-Covid world). In many cases, this computer-generated autoreply serves little purpose, especially when the recipient sends an email back a few minutes later. I recommend using out-of-office replies sparingly.

I knew a coworker who programmed his email to always respond with an out-of-office message that included his entire weekly schedule. This is what his out-of-office reply looked like:

"Here is my schedule for this week:

Mon: Cincinnati, OH Wholesaler

Tues: Travel

Wed: Columbus, OH Wholesaler

Thurs: Working from home

Fri: Detroit, MI Retailer Meeting"

The problem was that no one cared about his daily schedule.

When I email someone, I want an answer to my question, not an itinerary of someone's life plans. He was essentially spamming everyone who sent him an email.

Out-of-office replies are only valuable when they a) notify contacts that you truly are away from work and will not be checking your email throughout the day and b) provide the sender a backup contact in case of an urgent request.

Here is when I have used an out-of-office reply:

- On my honeymoon. (Hopefully, I will not have another one.)
- On vacation with my family, during which I was not checking email.
- When in the hospital for a surgery that required an overnight stay.
- On extended parental leave.

Here is when I do not use an out-of-office reply:

- If I'm traveling for business.
- When I'm taking vacation days at home and will be periodically checking email.
- During a company holiday.

Wasted emails can come in all shapes and sizes. Most of the time, the size is one word. Don't flood inboxes with wasted emails that provide little information and value. When you don't send wasted emails, you show that you respect your coworkers' time and energy. You also demonstrate that, when you do send a message, it contains information of value.

PAUSE BEFORE HITTING SEND

Before you hit send, pause and double-check your work. Check for errors in your messages. Ensure that what you're sending is correct. I've caught many mistakes during a final review before hitting send.

At a minimum, reread what you wrote before hitting send. Sometimes, small grammatical errors can completely obscure the meaning of a message. If your message has an attachment, make sure the attachment is attached! Also, before you hit send, open the attachment. Make sure it is the correct attachment. And review the attachment for errors. Here are other things you should double-check before hitting send:

- you provided all the requested information
- the message is addressed to the correct person
- a forwarded message chain does not contain information that should not be disclosed to your recipient

If you can edit messages after you send them, such as in Slack, take advantage of this feature, and correct any mistakes you find (especially if the recipient has yet to respond). If you do notice a consequential error in an already delivered email, notify the recipient of your mistake, and send the corrected information. For example, if I see an error in an emailed Excel file—even if it is later in the day—I resend a corrected copy.

Don't be too quick to click send. When you send a message that is not clear or submit an assignment that is incorrect, you're giving more work to your recipient, especially if your customer has to ask for clarification or your boss needs to correct your errors. Still, if your message contains mistakes, it's not the end of the world. I've made all the above mistakes and more. Just don't be the person who habitually has errors in their messages. The key is to learn from your mistakes and continually try to improve.

KNOW WHEN EMAIL IS NOT ENOUGH

To get things done, you need to know when an email just isn't cutting it. A pet peeve of mine is when I hear "I sent them a message, but they didn't get back to me. So, I don't know the answer." If someone is not getting back to you, don't be afraid to pick up the phone. If you need a response and your messages are unanswered, pick up the phone and make an old-fashioned call.

Telephoning can often be better than messaging when dealing with complicated issues. If an email will take at least three minutes to read, I recommend calling to discuss the issue rather than sending a message. You are often able to resolve problems much faster if you talk through them in real-time versus having to message back and forth a handful of times. Many people actually prefer to talk rather than try to dissect and respond via long, complex messages.

Before making a call, I often message or text the person to see if they are available to talk. We may end up talking then or scheduling a time to talk later. Telephone conversations can be followed up with an email that summarizes what was discussed and anything agreed upon during the conversation. It is always good to have an agreement made over the phone documented in writing.

Don't rely strictly on electronic messaging for communication. Recognize when messaging is just not cutting it and take advantage of all possible communication methods (i.e., phone, text, email, in-person meeting) to get the information you need when you need it. For urgent issues, my first line of communication is generally a telephone call.

Don't send one message and wait indefinitely. There's no magical formula for how long to wait before following up. Rather, the time for follow-up communication is when you need information and you don't have it.

When your messages are going unanswered or if you need to discuss a particularly complicated matter, it's time to pick up the phone and make a call. To be effective in getting things done, you need to know when email is not enough.

RECAP

Your messages are an extension of you, so it is especially important that your messages are not an afterthought but managed with purpose and care. Remember to:

- respond to messages within the hour or, at most, within a day;

- keep your inbox in tip-top shape by using folders and deleting emails you do not need;

- make your emails clear and concise by using headings and bullet points;

- avoid cluttering your coworkers' inboxes with unnecessary thank-you and out-of-office emails; and

- pick up the phone if you don't get a response via email, and talk through the issue in real-time.

When you show that you can manage the small things, like your messages, it signals that you can handle the big things, too.

CHAPTER 3

STUDY FOR SUCCESS

THE EXPERTISE NEEDED to advance your career isn't going to come naturally. You are going to have to study for success. Just as studying outside of regular class time helped you excel in school, spending extra time studying job-related competencies will help you in your career. The key is to be strategic. In other words, study smarter rather than harder (as the saying goes). Focus on the things you use and are asked about daily. With this in mind, I recommend studying Microsoft Excel, job-related statistics, and key talking points. Strengthening your skills in these areas will provide the most return on your time and energy investments.

EXCEL IN EXCEL

If I could share only one piece of business advice, it would be to *excel in Excel*. In the business sector, most jobs involve working with and manipulating data in spreadsheets. Being able to proficiently read a spreadsheet, manipulate data, and create your own reports is essential. When you can do these things independently, rather than relying on others, you can respond quickly to questions and requests for information.

Some companies are transitioning from relying solely on

Excel for their analytics. If your company uses a data analytics application other than Excel, such as Google Sheets, become proficient in that application! Still, Excel remains the primary analytics tool used by many businesses. Many of today's finance and business executives grew up with and still rely on Excel. It is often entrenched within company protocols, and monthly usage of Excel continues to grow year over year.[1]

If you're between jobs and looking to take a data analytics course, you won't go wrong with strengthening your Excel skills. If you're looking to improve your Excel skills and aren't sure where to begin, these are basic Excel skills I like my employees to possess:

- The ability to create charts and pivot tables
- The ability to use conditional formatting
- The ability to write formulas like SUMIF statements and VLOOKUP

These are the more advanced skills I like to see:

- The ability to calculate correlation
- The ability to perform a regression analysis
- The ability to write and run macros
- The ability to write VBA (Visual Basic for Applications) coding

Many people think that because they took a college course on Excel, they know how to use the tool. However, in those classes, you're using fake data like widgets. Even tutorials on YouTube and self-help books only describe general scenarios. Using Excel with real data is much different.

Becoming an expert in Excel takes years and years of on-the-job experience. I thought I was an expert in Excel until I worked with my second boss in Bentonville. I was blown away by what he knew and what I didn't. I spent at least a full year sitting with him for a few hours a week, and I learned as much as I could about what he did in Excel and Microsoft Access. No training course or college class could have taught me what I learned from sitting with an expert. I strongly recommend shadowing coworkers who are experts in Excel to strengthen your Excel skills.

The shadowing process may seem intimidating, especially if you are worried about imposing on others. Here are some steps to help you with the process:

- Find an Excel expert by asking around or checking to see who authored the complex Excel reports you receive.

- Inform that person you would like to get better at Excel and are looking for pointers and tricks. (I have found that most of the time, Excel experts enjoy sharing their knowledge and helping others improve their skills.)

- Ask if you can sit with and observe them the next time they create an Excel report. Hopefully, they will talk you through how they constructed the report and the reasoning behind their choices.

- If sitting with an expert is not an option, ask them what their most frequently used or most helpful formulas are. Then, watch YouTube videos on how to use those formulas.

Another way to strengthen your Excel skills is by replicating completed reports. Earlier in my career, when I received an amazing Excel report (one with dropdown boxes and complex formulas), I regularly tried during my downtime to mimic the report using the same raw data. This typically involved a mix of trial and error as well as assistance from others. After replicating the report, I then attempted to improve it. I might have added dropdowns to streamline the data entry process or created additional charts to improve interpretability. You could also try to find two existing reports that can be combined to reduce redundancy.* Not only will this strengthen your Excel skills, but it will also help your company and wow your bosses.

Being proficient in your company's data manipulation software, whether it be Excel or another application, is one of the most important business skills. Still, becoming an expert in Excel doesn't happen overnight. It can take years of on-the-job practice and mentoring. Once you can excel in Excel, you can more easily provide your team with information and assistance.

I want people on my team who are proficient in understanding and analyzing data. And, when I look for people to promote, I choose people who excel in Excel.

KNOW YOUR NUMBERS

When I rattle off statistics, people often assume I know much more than I actually do. And industry experts agree that using numbers and statistics can make you look more knowledgeable.[2] Accordingly, I recommend studying and memorizing job-relevant

---

*As more people join your team, more and more reports are typically created, since people like to have different numbers available or have personal preferences for how their numbers are laid out. Accordingly, I try to condense reports every year to reduce redundancy, which inevitably occurs over time.

statistics and using them when speaking to customers and coworkers.

I remember being on a market visit with Target's Alcohol team when I was Category Management Director for National Grocery Stores with A-B.* During this tour, I shared some statistics with the Target team:

- The average beer display provides a 30% lift.**[3]

- The average shopper spends thirty seconds in the beer aisle.

- The most common item purchased with beer is bananas.***[4]

The Target team was impressed. Every time I met with them over the next few years, they talked about how I knew *every* number and even mentioned it to my boss on multiple occasions—obviously, a plus. Target also chose A-B for Beverage Supplier of the Year both years I worked with their Beer Category. This probably wasn't due solely to me wowing them with numbers, but I'm sure it didn't hurt.

I recommend learning a small subset of numbers very well so you can quote this data in conversation. I suggest focusing on key numbers most applicable to your particular area. For example, if you manage sales for the entire United States, make sure you know

---

*On a market visit, we walk through the stores of multiple retailers to see how each store merchandises their products on the shelf, what items are on displays, and how the entire store is organized.

**_Lift_ refers to an increase in sales from advertising or promotion and is used to measure marketing effectiveness. To calculate lift you need to compare sales during the promotional period to baseline data.

***Bananas are typically the most common item purchased in a grocery store. So, the most common item purchased with [replace "beer" with pretty much any food item] is bananas.

your sales numbers for the entire country, your top-performing state, and your worst-performing state. If you manage sales for a specific state, know stats for your biggest, fastest-growing, and fastest-declining markets. Try to anticipate what numbers you may be asked for and learn those numbers.

It is also crucial that you know the numbers associated with your goals. KPIs (**key performance indicators**) are goals stated in quantitative terms. For example, the KPIs for a beverage company's sales team may be:

- achieve 75% distribution of an item; and

- grow market share by 1%.

Typically in business, employees' performance evaluations are impacted (at least in part) by how well they met their individual and/or teams' KPIs. Most bonuses are influenced by individual KPI performance together with overall company performance. Accordingly, you must be able to speak fluently about your KPI numbers—for example, during your monthly performance review with your boss. (For more information about knowing your KPIs, see Practice Your Elevator Speech.)

To really know your numbers, you're going to have to study. Try setting aside at least fifteen minutes every week to review your numbers. Then, start using your memorized numbers on the job. Even if you are not asked, bring up your memorized numbers in everyday conversation. This will help you remember the data and allow you to practice communicating fluently. If you manage a team, ask them questions about their stats during weekly team meetings. You will encourage your team to know their numbers, and you will gain business information through the process.

When I first started at Gopuff, my boss held a meeting every Monday afternoon with our merchandising team to review the previous week's sales. He typically asked questions like "What were the total Snacks sales last week?" or "What new item had the best results?" To his frustration, it was not unusual for these questions to go unanswered. During one meeting, he tried an unconventional approach. He put $100 on the table for anyone who could answer all of his next five questions. No one could. During the next Monday meeting, everyone came prepared to talk about sales performance with the hopes of becoming $100 richer. He threw the $100 down again. But even with preparation, no one was able to answer every question. The moral of this story isn't that learning your numbers is impossible. Instead, it exemplifies that my boss was trying to do everything in his power to motivate his team to know their numbers.

What is just as important as knowing your numbers by heart is knowing where to find the numbers when you need them. Throughout my career, I have regularly received calls from my boss asking for specific numbers. Most of the time, I was able to provide an answer right away. I hated saying, "I will get back to you," because I felt like that made me look like I didn't know my business. When my Walmart Beer Buyer called asking for specific information, I sometimes was able to pull the data from the database, analyze it, and send him the key points while he was still on the phone. He saw this as customer service at its best.

While you aren't usually expected to provide numbers within seconds, it is common for customers and senior management to want numbers ASAP. Many of these ASAP requests simply require you to look at a particular report. Accordingly, I recommend keeping your reports organized in one folder on your computer. If your reports are on digital dashboards, make sure the links are easily accessible so you can access them quickly. Since some requests necessitate calculations from multiple reports, you should also know how to manipulate data, as discussed in the excelling in Excel section. In sum, know how to access data. You don't want to spend hours figuring out how to find it or waiting on others to do it for you when you receive a request.

Know your numbers. While you don't need to know every number, you do need to know the numbers that matter. And it also can't hurt knowing some that don't. Study your numbers and practice reciting them. Since it is impossible to memorize all of your numbers, be comfortable pulling and analyzing your own data so you can respond quickly to requests. When you know your numbers or, at least, know how to get the numbers you need, you can stand out by helping your coworkers and customers get the information they need promptly. Knowing your numbers is a great way to wow your customer and your boss and show that you have what it takes to be promoted.

PRACTICE YOUR ELEVATOR SPEECH

At different times throughout my career, I have run into company executives who (probably to make small talk) asked me something like "What are you working on?" In situations like these, it would be easy to impulsively respond, "I'm so busy," and only mention what I happened to be working on at that exact moment. However, would a comment like that be memorable, help me stand out, or leave the executive wanting to know more about me and what I'm working on?

Whether an executive asks, "How are you?" or "What are you

working on?," it's vital that you don't say "I'm good" or "I'm busy" and give them an excuse to walk away. If someone asks what I am working on, I need to be prepared to mention the most innovative, ground-breaking project that will drive significant results for my company. I recommend that you prepare for a thirty-second to two-minute speech about your performance, your team's performance, or any big projects you are working on. I call these speeches "elevator speeches."

Make sure you're prepared to provide an elevator speech that will not only wow the executive but will get them asking more questions about what you just said. You need to reel them in. There have been times when what I said was so intriguing that the executive scheduled a meeting with me to discuss it in more detail.

Elevator speeches aren't just for your company's senior executives. You can use elevator speeches when talking to your boss, the manager of another department, or anyone within (or outside of) your company who could impact your career trajectory.

Here are some examples of topics you should be ready to discuss:

- A high-priority item you're working on.

  - *"We're making sure next week's New Year's Eve promotion launches without a hitch."*

- Something that will make them go "wow," such as an amazing stat you uncovered.

  - *"We just added this new chocolate potato chip to my assortment, and it is already my number five overall salty snack in dollars."*

- An immediate issue or challenge. (Don't make this a complaining session, but if an issue is about to get bad, share your situation, how you got there, and what you need to resolve it.)

  - *"We just found out our new Teavana cans will have a delayed start date due to the can's color not matching the original specification. We are working with the manufacturer to get it corrected and are trying not to miss our launch date. We have already notified our retailers of this issue just in case we are one week late on launch."*

- The statistic that most positively highlights company performance.

  - *"Teavana is the number one selling Premium Ready-to-Drink Tea in rate of sale and more than two times bigger than our next biggest competitor."*

- The status of your personal key performance indicators (KPIs).

  - *"I'm achieving all but one of my KPIs. I'm falling short on my distribution KPI by five percent. Here is my plan to get back on track . . ."*

- Useful news about your competition.

  - *"I just read that this new retailer, LaLa Mart, launched in San Antonio and is delivering all of their items by drone."*

- The amount of revenue you will deliver this year for your company and your projection for next year.

○ *"Our alcohol business is projected to grow by fifty percent this year, from ten million last year to fifteen million this year. This is driven by strong growth from hard seltzers, sparkling wine, and tequila."*

Also, be prepared for any frequently asked questions. When I managed Teavana Ready-to-Drink Iced Tea, "What is your projection for Teavana's total dollar sales this year?" had to be the question I received most often from senior management. If you're not in sales, ask yourself what is the number one metric your management cares about and may inquire about?

I suggest you write out the answers to these questions and practice reciting them from memory. (Knowing your numbers is an integral part of pulling off a great elevator speech.) The more prepared you are, the more confident you will sound and the more on-point your information will be. If I'm traveling with or know I will be spending time with senior leadership or my boss, I work a little harder to prepare for these speeches.

An opportunity for an elevator speech will not necessarily happen in an elevator. It could be in the breakroom, the bathroom, or on your way out the door when leaving work. It could be while waiting at the airport or during the ride to the hotel or meeting. It also could be during a virtual call when, after you're done speaking about a specific issue, you are asked, "What else is going on?" These non-meetings, while short, are ideal times to showcase your performance or the projects you are working on. These are opportunities to sell yourself.

You only get so many chances to chat with your company's senior employees, and these impromptu moments can happen without warning. If you're unprepared, you will most likely come up with a generic response or have no response if you freeze up and can't think of anything to say. This is unfortunate. Getting facetime with a high-level executive, while likely infrequent, can positively impact your career. So, regardless of whether the interaction is in person, virtual, or on the phone, if you have individual time with your management, make it count. When asked a question, you won't have time to say, "Hold on, let me get my notes." You need to be prepared to speak on the spot. The moment you're asked, "What's going on?" and you say, "Nothing," you've just failed to stand out. So, practice your elevator speech and be prepared to show—within a moment's notice—that you have what it takes to be promoted.

RECAP

To increase your chances of getting promoted, take time out of your schedule to study things that will take your career to the next level. Make study time count by focusing on these general goals:

- Become proficient in Microsoft Excel. You may think you know how to use Excel, but there is likely room for improvement.

- Memorize job-specific numbers and statistics so you can confidently include these points when speaking with others. While you don't need to know every number by heart, you do need to know how to find the numbers you may be asked about.

- Practice an elevator speech. Prepare how you would answer an array of prompts should you be given the unexpected (or expected) opportunity to speak with a high-level executive. You don't want to find yourself unprepared to take advantage of an opportunity to showcase how you add value to your company.

Having a minimum amount of proficiency or knowledge is never enough. Challenge yourself to study more, learn more, and know more. Study for success so you will always be ready to show you have what it takes to be promoted.

CHAPTER 4

TAKE CONTROL OF YOUR DAY

ALL TOO OFTEN, we relinquish control over what happens during our day without even realizing it. We let others take charge of whether or not meetings happen, haphazardly schedule appointments into our first available slots, and squeeze in time to work on our most important projects rather than making them a priority—all while continuously accomplishing less than expected.

It's time to break away from inefficient habits. It's time to stop being passive and complacent about your workday and take control of your day, your time, and your career.

In this chapter, I focus on how to create workdays that allow for short-term time management and long-term career growth. In Make Your Own Meetings, I highlight the importance of scheduling meetings with important persons within your company and provide tips on making those meetings as productive and powerful as possible. In Be a Strategic Scheduler, I provide recommendations on how to create an intentional, personalized schedule that enables you to do your best work. Finally, in Keep Up to Date on the Road, I go over how to stay on top of your work when traveling for business. As you make small changes in how you approach your day, you will feel more in control, productive, and capable of finding even more ways to optimize your time. So, get ready to take control of your career by taking control of your day.

MAKE YOUR OWN MEETINGS

Take the initiative to create meetings with people who can help you get promoted. Regular communication with your boss, for example, is an important step in getting promoted. You need to find one-on-one time to provide updates, discuss your performance, share ideas, and establish a strong relationship. If you simply sit back and wait for meetings to be scheduled for you, you could be missing out on crucial opportunities to help your career. Be proactive about getting face time.

ONE-ON-ONES

One-on-one time between you and your boss is extremely valuable. As a manager, I get to know my direct reports best during one-on-one meetings. The better I understand someone's strengths, the better I can choose and delegate projects that build upon their talents and enable them to excel and display exceptional performance. As a direct report myself, I look forward to one-on-one meetings with my boss, as this is my personal time to showcase my work and strengthen our relationship.

I recommend scheduling weekly one-on-one meetings with your boss. Make sure these meetings are on both of your calendars. And, if conflicts arise, find another time during that week to meet. When my team and I worked in the office, I had one-on-one meetings with my direct reports once a week. These meetings were in addition to mini conversations that we had throughout the day when we all sat near each other.

When we worked remotely, I told my direct reports that I was available to meet with them one-on-one twice per week to review projects, get help with something they were working on, or discuss their performance. I also informed them that if they wanted to take me up on this offer, it was up to them to schedule the meeting. So far, 100% of my team has been scheduling meetings with me two times a week.

I now prefer two thirty-minute meetings over one sixty-minute meeting, especially when the two meetings are spread out during the week. This allows for more conversation throughout the week, which is especially helpful when working on those projects which benefit from frequent feedback and assistance.

I emphasize to my direct reports that these one-on-one meetings are *their* meetings, and it's up to them to bring up what they want to discuss. If my direct report says they don't have anything to talk about, that's on them. Some employees come with no agenda, and the meeting lasts five minutes. In contrast, others come prepared with a full agenda of what they would like to talk about, and the session lasts for thirty minutes. Which meetings do you think are more helpful and productive? Which employees do you think look ready to be promoted?

I recommend coming prepared to one-on-one meetings with a list of items to discuss. Trying to think of things on the fly is not a good strategy and can waste time. When I meet with my boss, I prepare a list of topics to discuss. I focus on the most important and time-sensitive topics first and bring up additional items if time allows. Remember, one-on-one meetings are one of the few times you can share anything without coworkers present, so be deliberate with your time.

Don't let your one-on-one meeting (or any meeting) turn into a complaining session. This can happen when you only talk about problems and not solutions. When bringing up a difficulty, don't solely rely on your boss to come up with a fix. Instead, come prepared with potential solutions to your problems and clarify how your boss can be of assistance.

If your boss is not interested in meeting weekly or regularly, then find excuses to meet by asking to talk about a specific project. Talk about that project at the beginning of the meeting, and save some time to discuss additional items, such as a best practice you're developing. Don't let your boss's weaknesses stop you from receiving the guidance and feedback you need to perform your job well.

It is also valuable to get facetime with leaders above your boss. Your boss's boss is a crucial person to get to know, as they may be one of the people needed to approve your future promotion. I actually like and appreciate it when people say, "I would like to meet with you *and* your boss about this new project."

OTHER DEPARTMENT HEADS

Maintaining communication with cross-functional employees and heads of other departments is also advantageous. If there are people on other teams who should be in the loop about what you're doing, don't just wait for someone else to facilitate communication between you and the other departments. Instead, communicate with them directly. The strongest employees make it known when they're working on a big project.

The more employees who know what you're working on and how they can be of support, the more support you will receive and the more successful you will be. Working in a silo is not going to get you far. It is very hard to get support if you are not sharing.

As the Merchandising Director of Alcohol at Gopuff, I had to ensure that multiple cross-functional teams (i.e., Marketing, Customer Relationship Management [CRM], Digital Merchandising, Supply, Operations, Go to Market) were all in the loop about my projects and knew how they could support my initiatives. For example, if the Alcohol team did a special partnership with an alcohol brand endorsed by a high-profile celebrity, I worked with other departments to ensure prioritization on the app and that the product was promoted through email, social media, and in-app messaging.

The more people who know what you're working on, the more likely your name will be brought up in conversation. Soon, others will want to initiate meetings with you. Make your own meetings with employees from other teams and departments, especially when working on a project that requires cross-functional support.

UPRISERS AND NEW HIRES

I also recommend reaching out to talented employees who are rising within the company. I call employees who seem on a fast track to many promotions "uprisers." Identifying and building a positive rapport with uprisers can be a career asset, especially if they get promoted faster than you. If you have a good relationship with uprisers, as they get promoted to new teams or departments, they can keep you in the loop, bring you up in conversation, and even contribute to your promotion by speaking highly about you or hiring you onto their teams.

I also try to schedule a meeting with any new employees in senior roles with which I collaborate. I introduce myself and talk about relevant past and present projects. Most of the time, no one instructs me to have this meeting, nor is it something scheduled by HR or another employee. It is me reaching out to the person and recommending that we come up with a time to talk about how we can work together.

LEADERSHIP TEAM—AT THE GYM!

Depending on your level within the company, it may be appropriate to also get to know your company's leadership team. This is particularly beneficial if your boss or boss's boss are on the leadership team. (The leadership team is typically made up of employees who report to the CEO or founder and oversee one or multiple departments within the organization.) Being known among this group is an asset, as they typically approve incremental bonuses for select employees and award Employee of the Year.

Take advantage of any opportunity or invitation from your CEO to meet. For example, many CEOs tell their employees during town hall meetings that they have an open-door policy and invite employees to share with them any ideas about how to grow the business. Take them up on this offer! At A-B, I scheduled a one-on-one meeting with our global CEO. During our thirty-minute meeting, I shared some big ideas and discussed future roles I was interested in. At the end of the meeting, he told me that he appreciated me for scheduling the meeting and to set up another meeting in six months.

Never shy away from opportunities to get to know or speak with senior-level executives, even if the occasion seems a bit unconventional. I remember being at a three-day A-B wholesaler meeting in St. Louis with about 150 attendees. On the third (and last) day of the conference, I woke up early and headed to the hotel gym. (Typically, the first morning of a conference will have the most employees working out. The second morning will have about half as many as the first. By the last day, you are lucky to see five employees.)

On this particular morning at the gym, it was initially just the guy running the meeting and me. Over the next twenty minutes, in came our CEO, President, and Head of the High End Business Unit. We didn't talk much in the gym. However, I strategically left the gym at the same time as our CEO and spoke with him for a few minutes while walking to the elevator.

I have found the hotel gym during business conferences to be a great place to run into senior-level executives. In fact, I saw every one of my last six A-B bosses there multiple times. Regardless of whether you have a short discussion or you don't even end up talking, you will both remember when you see each other later in the day that you have something in common. While most people were trying to get an extra hour of sleep, you both made the commitment to wake up early and put your body to work. Even if you don't run into a high-level executive at the gym, connecting with other coworkers (and exercising) also counts as a win.

INFORMAL CHATS

Don't limit communication to formally scheduled meetings. Take advantage of times between formal meetings to share information. At the office, there are typically numerous opportunities for conversation—at your desk, in passing, at lunch, and after meetings. You may be asking yourself, "Does my boss really want me to talk to them in the breakroom?" As a manager myself, I want to be as knowledgeable as possible about my employees and the business. So, if I get any tidbits of info outside of meetings, that works for me.

When working remotely, you miss out on those five-minute ad hoc conversations within an office and have to make up for that time. Accordingly, put extra effort into carving out opportunities to connect with your boss and coworkers. One way to do this is by increasing everyday communication through Slack, email, text, and phone. I do my best to stay connected to my team, even if it is just with a quick message to see how someone is doing.

There are usually many opportunities for informal meetings when traveling for business. If I am traveling with my boss, I prepare a list of questions and information I want to mention. Then, I try to find time to talk, like at the airport or in the car ride to our meeting or hotel. The caution here is to make sure you don't talk business all the time, especially when traveling. It can get annoying if all your conversations revolve around work.

You don't want to always rely on others to initiate meetings. If you think a meeting would be helpful, do your best to make it happen. Be sure to have regular one-on-one meetings with your boss and make these meetings as productive as possible. Also, go out of your way to schedule meetings with your boss's boss, persons in cross-functional teams and departments, and rising stars in the company. Take advantage of invitations from your senior leaders to present ideas and try to make an impression. When you take the initiative to make your own meetings, you're taking control of your day and your career.

BE A STRATEGIC SCHEDULER

During the beginning months of the pandemic, Gopuff's sales sky-rocketed. We were busier than ever. Although we were still adjusting to working from home, I needed my team to remain committed to and focused on getting their work done. Working outside the office proved more difficult for some employees than others.

One of my direct reports lived in an apartment with roommates and found working from home particularly challenging. Initially, he struggled with a lack of workspace, his roommates being too loud, and spotty internet. It soon became clear that these environmental obstacles were only part of the problem. Time management was also an issue. Together, we worked on how he could be more intentional and deliberate with his schedule to be more productive.

Most people don't think twice about when they schedule a meeting or answer an email. They typically plan a meeting during their first available opening, use their time outside meetings to respond to emails, and work on long-term projects with whatever time is left over. This is the default approach and how I typically function if I'm not being intentional with my time.

While you can get by with an arbitrary work schedule, implementing the recommendations in this book requires deliberate use of your time. You need to be conscious of and strategic with your time to increase productivity and improve performance.

A key to managing time effectively is being strategic about when you do certain tasks. For example, I am a morning person. I am most energetic, focused, and productive in the morning. Accordingly, if I have intellectually demanding work to do (like analyzing a complicated data set), I prefer to do this work at the beginning of my day. I avoid scheduling calls in the morning to make this happen and block out segments of my schedule to work on these complex, analytical tasks. I learned from Daniel H. Pink's book *When: The Scientific Secrets of Perfect Timing* that research shows that, in general, the best time to do complex tasks is in the morning, when most people tend to be alert and focused.[1]

On the flip side, I have lower energy in the afternoon. Three p.m. is my dead zone. This is the time when, if there were a bed right next to my desk, I would be lying in it. If I attempt to do analytical work after lunch, it will take me longer, and I am bound to make more mistakes. Again, I'm not alone here. Research shows that energy levels and alertness for most people max out in the late morning to noon hours and sharply decline in the afternoon.[2] Therefore, I try to schedule calls and meetings in the afternoon during my dead zone. I used to have my daily team meeting at three p.m. I didn't sleep through my team meetings. Rather, interacting with others counteracted my tiredness and gave me a second wind.

Being less alert in the afternoon isn't all bad. Pink shared that most people do their best creative or insight-oriented work in the afternoon, when they're not as focused and are less likely to edit away new or alternative ideas.[3]

Still, one type of schedule will not be perfect for everyone. People vary in their physiological makeups and circadian rhythms. For example, at least 20% of people are "night owls." A night owl's cognitive performance improves as the day progresses, peaking in the late afternoon or early evening.[4] Thus, it is important to understand your personal circadian rhythm *and* the demands of particular tasks when creating your ideal schedule.

Another key to strategic scheduling is knowing how to take a good break. A large body of research shows a breadth of benefits from taking breaks. Breaks improve mental stamina and counteract cognitive declines that naturally occur for most people in the afternoon.[5]

Still, not all breaks are created equal. Pink explained that the best and most effective breaks involve moving around, being social, and going outside. If a break includes two or three of these characteristics, even better.[6] And don't feel the need to talk or think about work during your breaks. Research shows that completely detaching from work during breaks increases their effectiveness.[7]

Walking outside with a coworker can make for a very effective break. If you don't work around others, try meeting up with a friend for coffee or lunch. When I worked in an office, I almost always went out to lunch. (I'm a food person and enjoy going out to eat, especially when working in NYC.) It was even better if I could find one or more coworkers to go with me. I didn't know it at the time, but these lunches align with what research identifies as the most effective breaks because they got me away from my work, outside, moving around, and socializing with others!

When I started working from home during the pandemic, breaks and lunch looked different from in the office. I soon realized that, since I was not traveling to meeting rooms and was now just steps away from the bathroom, I walked significantly less. So, during breaks at home, I try to walk around the house, go up and down the stairs, step outside, or even play five minutes of basketball. Since I don't typically go out to lunch when working from home, I like to eat lunch outside my office and watch TV or talk to my wife rather than do work-related things while eating.

So, whether you're at the office or working from home, don't be ashamed to take breaks. Breaks are a strategic component of an efficient and productive day.

To recap, plan out your daily schedule with intention and

purpose. Be strategic and create a strategy that plays to your natural capabilities, job responsibilities, and particular circumstances instead of just letting your schedule "happen." For my direct report who had difficulty adapting to remote work, strategic scheduling meant dedicating blocks of time in his schedule to specific projects. For others, it may mean scheduling complex thinking tasks in the morning and tasks that require creativity in the afternoon. Regardless of what specific schedule works for you, take breaks that allow you to step away from your work and energize yourself. You will get the most out of your day and yourself when you take control of your schedule.

KEEP UP TO DATE ON THE ROAD

When some employees travel for business, I have noticed that they forget about doing their normal job. Some people don't answer one email when they travel and then spend their entire first day back in the office catching up. This is not a good strategy. Your normal work doesn't stop when you're away for business. You need to know how to balance travel and work.

During my final six years with A-B, I spent over 50% of my work time traveling. It can be fun to experience different places, people, and food. However, driving for long hours, waiting at airports, squeezing into airplane seats, and sleeping in uncomfortable beds can become exhausting. When you add your regular work to everything involved with being on the road, it's understandable that many people have trouble staying on top of their work when away.

It's hard to maintain your work routine and easy to fall behind when on the road. A portion of your day is usually spent traveling and in extra meetings, all while receiving the same number of emails, project requests—you name it. Accordingly, when I travel, it is imperative that I plan my days more carefully and use my time efficiently to avoid falling behind. You can stay on top of things if you are very conscientious and diligent with your time. Here are some strategies to help you keep up to date when you're on the road.

First, find ways to take advantage of the full day. As discussed in the section on scheduling, it is advantageous to take advantage of periods of the day when you feel most alert to get things done. This could be early in the morning at a hotel, at night after dinner, or at a coffee shop during the day. While traveling, I find early mornings to be my most productive time. Since I don't usually have a long morning commute, I typically have extra time in the morning (even after going to the hotel gym) and use this precious time to catch up on work.

Second, find a good spot to work. Finding a good place to work while on the road can often take some creativity. When traveling for A-B, if I was in an area with a regional office, I tried to work from there since I knew the Internet connection would be strong and I would have access to office supplies. (At a regional office, I also had the potential to have impromptu discussions with coworkers whom I didn't normally see.) So, whatever your particular situation, consider: Where will you have Wi-Fi? Where is it quiet? In what type of environment do you tend to stay alert and focused? Don't be afraid to think outside the box. Also, try to plan ahead so you don't waste too much of your day figuring out where to work.

If I'm traveling by car, I sometimes make telephone calls (hands-free) while driving. During my weekly commute to Bentonville, Arkansas, from St. Louis, when I managed Walmart Sales for A-B, I enjoyed randomly calling people on my team to ask how they were doing. (I recommend this only if the route is familiar and not mentally demanding, such as my five-hour drive through Missouri that I made twice a week for multiple years.) During the drive, I was able to help team members, strengthen our working relationships, and learn more about our business from them.

I try to make the most of my time when traveling by airplane. While I do need to be extra cautious when working on sensitive information in the close quarters of a plane, I enjoy being able to work without distraction from incoming messages, calls, and coworkers. In fact, I find plane rides to be a great time to work on presentations. Catching up on emails is also easy for me to do on a plane. Even without Wi-Fi, I can usually read and write responses, which are then automatically sent when my device connects to the Internet. Don't let a temporary lack in Wi-Fi keep you from being productive.

Find a strategy that works for you, and don't let traveling be an excuse or the reason you get behind. You need to demonstrate that you can stay on top of your work, whatever the situation.

By taking control of your day, even while on the road, you demonstrate that you can handle whatever is put in front of you— including a promotion.

RECAP

In order to effectively manage your time, you must take control of when things happen. Do these things to take control of your day:

- Take the initiative to create your own meetings and prepare for those meetings to get the most out of them.

Don't wait for others to schedule meetings or bring up important issues.

- Be purposeful about when you schedule tasks. Take into consideration when you are most alert and when you need a break to be productive.

- Stay up to date when you're traveling. Be extra deliberate and strategic with your time while on the road to avoid getting behind.

When you take control of your day, you take control of your future.

CHAPTER 5

HELP YOUR TEAM SUCCEED

WE ALL WANT TO DO WELL and be recognized for our work. However, when you attempt to get that recognition through competing with, outdoing, or putting down your coworkers (no matter how sly you think you are), people notice, and this negatively impacts your career. Instead of trying to outdo your coworkers, focus on helping and supporting them. When you help your team succeed, you will ultimately receive the recognition you want and deserve.

Working with and supporting your team becomes more and more important as you move up in a company. In many entry-level positions, you are an individual contributor. You are given tasks and work on your own to complete them. However, as you move up in a company, you typically rely on a team to complete increased amounts of work. If you are a manager, your performance is likely tied to the performance of your team. Accordingly, you must be able to work effectively with your team and contribute to its success.

In this chapter, I outline how to become an essential part of a successful team. These strategies include using "we" instead of "I," being positive, adding to discussions, asking for help, learning from your mistakes, taking responsibility for your actions, and acting as a team leader. When you do these things, you demonstrate you can work well in a team and contribute to that team's success. Now, let's learn how to help your team succeed because when your team succeeds, you succeed.

USE "WE" INSTEAD OF "I"

In *Trillion Dollar Coach: The Leadership Playbook of Silicon Valley's Bill Campbell*, we learn that former coach and businessman Bill Campbell sought to hire people who understood that their own success depended upon their company's success. He maintained that job candidates who tended to use "we" instead of "I" were like those players he encountered as a coach who put their team first and cheered on their team even when on the bench.[1] Like Bill Campbell, I, too, believe in the power of "we." Using language that reflects a "we" versus "me" mentality conveys that your team's success is just as or even more important than your own recognition.

I remember my first meeting with the Beer Buyer from a large grocery store chain called Meijer. I gave a presentation on how Anheuser-Busch could help his company manage its beer category more effectively. In my presentation, I kept saying "we" did this and "we" did that. Never once did I say, "I created this strategy." The Buyer didn't say anything to me about it at the time. A week later, he called me and said that he was impressed with the way I used "we" instead of "I." We ended up having a great working relationship over the next few years.

Since getting that feedback, I've used "we" in all my presentations and discussions—even if I did 100% of the work. Whether I am presenting or just talking, if I catch myself (as I often do) saying "I," I quickly stop, pause, go back, and say "we." It's as simple as that. When I listen to my team members give presentations and they say "I," I usually talk to them later about changing the "I" to "we." I also use "we" in emails. After I write an email, I often review it and change each "I" to "we."

Why does it matter? It's not just about demonstrating teamwork and synergy to external customers and associates. It's also, more importantly, about the impression you give of your team. When you use "we" instead of "I," you communicate to your team that you are not competing against them but working with them toward a common goal.

There are many times when you want to brag to your boss and talk about all the great things you did on your own. Believe me; I always want to showcase my talents and my worth to my boss. However, as a boss, one of my biggest turn-offs is to listen to a team member present a project that many people worked on and continually hear "I," "I," "I," as if there is no "we" in their vocabulary. Even if you believe you deserve all the credit, using "I" can backfire if it makes you look like you care more about touting your accomplishments than prioritizing working as a team to accomplish shared goals.

When communicating, I recommend saying "we did this" instead of "I did this." Using "we" instead of "I" helps foster a culture that prioritizes working together toward common objectives. I promote the people who use "we" because they reinforce team cohesiveness, collaboration, and success. I do not promote the "I" people. Nor do I advise colleagues to promote the "I" people. When you use "we" instead of "I," you show you want your team to succeed.

BE POSITIVE

Positivity at work is invaluable for employees wanting to be promoted. It's not enough to simply not be in a bad mood. It's important to do extra things that encourage and express positivity.

I once hired two recent college graduates, who we'll call Jeremy and Ashley, around the same time. On paper, they seemed equivalent. However, in practice, they were very different. Jeremy regularly made small asides and facial expressions that implied he felt annoyed and overburdened. He may have complained about a Friday meeting running late or let out a noticeable sigh after a project deadline was announced. I recognize that everyone has bad days, but these were not one-offs. Instead, this was every-day negativity that rubbed off on the team and rubbed off on me. I sometimes even dreaded giving him a project because I didn't want to hear him complain about it.

In comparison, I cannot remember Ashley making a single negative comment. She was a joy to work with. Whatever project I assigned her, no matter how dull, she seemed appreciative that she was given a project and excited to work on it. She viewed it as an opportunity to strengthen her skills. Ultimately, Ashley got promoted after nineteen months. It was her first promotion.

If I must pick between two people to promote and their work level is comparable, I'm going to pick the person I'd rather work with. And I'd rather work with a positive person.

Being positive is important because your positivity (and negativity) rubs off on your team and affects a team's overall per-formance. For example, if you are a manager who is regularly in a bad mood, your coworkers will be hesitant to talk to you. Your employee engagement will decline, and your team will not func-tion as effectively. In contrast, when you are positive, your energy is contagious and leads to increased energy, hope, creativity, participation, motivation, and commitment among your team.[2]

Still, you may be thinking, "Is it really possible to just *be* positive? What if someone is annoying me? What if I'm in a bad mood?" I agree that, by and large, we cannot just turn off our feelings, nor would it be healthy to continually do so. However, we can, to a certain degree, control what we do and say.

You can start being more positive by cutting down on negativity. Small negative comments, that you might dismiss as insignificant, can have a strong impact on others' emotions.[3] Here are some negative comments you may catch yourself saying and some alternative words to use instead:

Negative Statement	Positive Statement
That meeting sucked and was a waste of my time.	Let's make sure to send out an agenda prior to the next meeting, so I can see if it's relevant for me to attend.
We will never reach our sales budget.	Come on, team; let's keep grinding. Let's finish the year strong and build toward next year.
I can't work with that person anymore.	We seem to have different work and communication styles. I need to figure out how we can work together.
When will this meeting be over?	Let's focus on the biggest initiatives first and take the smaller initiatives offline.
I am not listening to what you are saying.	Can we set up a time to review this, so I can be sure to give it the attention it deserves? Right now, I am focusing on a big project due today.

Using positive statements, and refraining from negative ones, can have a big impact on your team. Researchers Marcial Losada and Emily Heaphy analyzed the dynamics of sixty teams in a large information-processing corporation as they developed their annual strategic plans. The highest-performing teams expressed more words of support, encouragement, and appreciation, such as "that's a good idea." These highest-performing teams made five to six positive statements for every negative statement spoken. This was significantly more positive statements than was seen in the medium- and low-performing teams. (The highest performing teams had 5.614 positive statements for every one negative statement. This is compared to 1.855 and 0.363 positive statements for every negative statement for the medium- and low-performing teams, respectively). These results are, interestingly, very similar to marital therapy research that shows couples in stable, happy marriages have five or more positive interactions for every negative one.[4] Losada and Heaphy concluded that positive and encouraging statements at work contribute to a dynamic that leads to higher-performing teams.[5]

To be positive, you don't have to go around being Mary Poppins all the time. There need to be some negative statements for a team to function effectively, such as when providing honest feedback about how we can improve. Also, a workplace benefits when employees feel comfortable expressing a full range of emotions with coworkers on their team or with whom they work closely.[6]

Instead of attempting to turn off your emotions, try to be aware of your emotions throughout the workday. Recognize when you're upset and handle negative emotion at work in professional and healthy ways, such as by taking a break or speaking one-on-one with a trusted colleague.[7] Also, try to monitor your verbal (and non-verbal) language to avoid making too many negative remarks. They are likely more impactful than you realize.

On numerous occasions, early in my career, my boss asked me, "What's wrong?" or "Why are you upset?" I typically replied, "Nothing's wrong." (Back then, I was honestly pretty oblivious to my own emotions and how I came across to others.*) Either right then or later, during private meetings, my boss let me know that I needed to work on being less visibly upset when receiving bad news and dealing with frustration. He explained that when a manager looks upset, the team notices. If you get down, it brings the team down. They lose confidence, and the whole team suffers. He said that sometimes it's in the team's best interest to hide how you're feeling.

Even though my boss provided me with this same feedback for multiple years, I still struggled. I continue to work on expressing positivity with my team. I try to make a habit of being extra positive to make up for those times when I inadvertently (or purposely) am harsh. If "negativity" is ever brought to your attention (like it was mine), don't be defensive. Take heed and make changes.

Being positive at work is an important component to getting promoted. Regardless of whether you are genuinely upset or just come across that way, a perceived negative attitude can be detrimental to your team's success and your individual career growth. Try not to make a habit of complaining. Stop yourself from making unnecessary negative remarks. Instead, find tactful and constructive ways to react to challenging situations.

Being positive helps your team. Being positive helps your organization. Being positive helps you.

---

*Many people, particularly young adults, are not well-attuned to their feelings. Emotional growth, potentially with the help of therapy, can help people get better at accurately identifying their emotions.

ADD VALUE

After being in school for most of our lives, it's understandable that people at work, especially early in their careers, often revert to how they behaved back in the classroom. You may view your boss as your teacher who asks questions with the intent of quizzing you or seeing how much you studied. Theoretically, your "teacher" should be able to continue with their "lesson" regardless of whether you raise your hand and speak up.

Sometimes you might refrain from speaking up too much and looking like a know-it-all. Other times you may speak up just enough to get your "participation points" (e.g., "I spoke up at the last meeting, so I can get away with not speaking at the next few"). While these strategies may have allowed you to succeed in high school, to advance within your company, you need to throw out this student–teacher mindset.

When you're at work, don't embody the role of a student who waits to be called on by the teacher. Your boss does not have a teacher's manual with all the answers. Your boss relies on you to come prepared, contribute, and help them. If you want to move to the "head of the class," speak up and add value at work.

I remember leading a Google Meets meeting with my team of fifteen people. I presented a proposed budget that included monthly sales projections for the rest of the year. I provided hypotheses for why some months may have higher sales based on seasonality, holidays, and promotional events. While I spoke, I hoped someone would chime in to let me know they agreed with my hypotheses or provide their own perspective. I spoke for ten minutes without a single contribution from my team. I finally asked, "Does anyone agree with me or have any thoughts?" (I was sharing my screen and couldn't see any non-verbal feedback.) No one responded, so I repeated the question. Finally, I called on one of my senior team members. After this person spoke, my other senior team member spoke up. While I appreciated their contributions, I was still disappointed.

I was not completely confident in my proposed budget. I was relying on my team to help me. In essence, this was their budget. This budget would determine my team's targets and criteria for their bonuses. I was hoping we would have had a more productive discussion between the whole team (not just the most senior members) about what the right budget would be. As a boss, I do not know all the answers. I hire people to help me. You are not helping or adding value when you stay silent.

The simplest way to add value is to provide input when asked. Whether it's a request for agenda items or an appeal for ideas during a brainstorming session, give them *something* when your boss asks you a question. As a manager, I prefer to sift through alternative options (good and bad) when decision-making rather than come up with all the options on my own. When my team can provide me with an array of alternatives, it saves me time and energy. In most cases, sharing an idea is better than not providing any input at all, even if the idea is not perfect.

Don't ignore emails, including group emails, asking for your input. Be sure to reply, even if it's a group email and others have already responded. Many times, I sent out requests for feedback to my team and then had to send follow-up emails one, two, or even three times before I got a response. This is time-consuming (as it often means first figuring out who did and did not respond and then sending out follow-up emails to those who haven't responded). When I send a request for feedback, I really want feedback. I'm not just sending out a note for people to read.

When you do not respond to requests for feedback, you are not adding value.

Being a good team member means adding your perspective even when you disagree with your boss or team. As a manager, I don't want to be surrounded by a team of people who constantly agree with me. I want team members who push back (tactfully), let me know when I'm wrong, and help me become better. It's okay to share that you agree with an idea, but don't default to this too often. Agreeing 100% of the time means you have nothing new to add or contribute.

You don't need to wait for information requests to add value. For example, a great time to speak up is when you come across something that doesn't make sense, like a certain process. I regularly tell my new hires at Gopuff to let me know if something we're doing seems backward or inefficient. New hires provide some of the best feedback because they offer a fresh set of eyes to flawed processes others have grown accustomed to.

Another way to proactively add value is through sharing business insights. This could be in the form of business-relevant articles or results from internal or external reports. Shoot your boss an email with "Hey, thought you might like to see this," and share what you found, whether a screenshot from an Excel file or a link to an article. Your boss will likely be appreciative, as it is impossible for anyone to keep up with all the emerging data, research, and news. Giving your boss new information or an image they can use in an upcoming meeting shows you are there to help your boss and your team.

It is important that you continually look for and take advantage of opportunities to add value, whether speaking up at meetings, replying to requests for feedback, or sharing business insights.

When you contribute your thoughts, opinions, and insights, you help your team and make their jobs easier. Your ideas don't have to be perfect. Different opinions spur discussion and can assist with decision-making. Don't underestimate the value you bring to the table. The people who add value are the people who stand out as ready to be promoted.

ASK FOR HELP

I remember when I tasked an analyst with creating a sales report in Excel. When I caught up with her at the end of the day, I learned that she had spent nearly the whole day Googling and watching YouTube videos to try to figure out how to do an Excel formula. She hadn't asked me for help because she "didn't want to bother" me. I told her, "From now on, send me a note or come talk to me if you can't figure out how to do something after ten minutes of trying. That's what I'm here for. I can't have you spending the whole day trying to figure one thing out."

When you're doing a project, if you don't know what to do, ask for help. I'd rather spend five minutes of my time helping you out than have you spend hours trying to figure out how to do something. (It is okay to try and figure things out by yourself, but be conscious of your time.)

Don't feel like you need to prove yourself by doing everything independently. When I assign projects, I usually expect my team members will reach out to other employees and take advantage of company resources. I actually prefer employees collaborate on projects, even if it means the project takes longer to complete. When work is divided and conquered, you often end up with a better result when additional minds and points of view are utilized.

If you're unclear about what exactly you're supposed to be doing for a project, ask. Sometimes I delegate a project and the person does the wrong thing. I'd rather take ten minutes of my time to clarify instructions than waste two hours redoing a project done incorrectly. Asking for help does not have to be a last resort. Consider asking for help when planning a project to make sure you're starting off on the right foot.

When you go to your boss for help, make their job easier by presenting them with potential solutions or courses of action. This shows you have tried to think through the issue and typically leads to a more productive conversation and better solutions.

Don't be afraid to ask for help. When you attempt to do everything by yourself, you give the appearance that you don't work well in teams, cannot delegate, are unable to work cross-functionally, and risk doing things incorrectly. Good team members and good leaders need to know how to ask for help. Demonstrate that you have what it takes to get promoted by asking for help.

ADMIT YOUR MISTAKES

After seeing a photo of a newly released beverage on Instagram, I wondered how it was selling on Gopuff, as I knew it was slated to be brought onto our platform. During a team meeting, I asked how this beverage was performing. Melissa, a category specialist, said she would look into it and get back to me. After a few hours, Melissa messaged me. "I made a mistake. When I set up the item [in Google Sheets], I didn't properly code the stores that would be taking the item. So, the item was never brought in [to the micro fulfillment centers]."

About a week later, during a team call, Melissa acknowledged the mistake and presented a new checks and balances system to ensure that all new items' locations would be properly coded. She had already received buy-in from the immediate team and was sharing the new process with the other team leaders and me.

While I was upset that the new items weren't brought in on time, I walked away from this situation thinking more favorably of Melissa, not less. I was very impressed with her for creating the new process, which gave me more confidence in our team's ability to work accurately moving forward.

We all make mistakes. However, most people don't want to admit their mistakes, especially if those mistakes negatively affect their company's business. They might worry they could lose out on a promotion—or lose their job—if their failure is made known.

Nevertheless, sharing failures can be good for you, your team, and your company. Research shows that the strongest teams are those that share failures. It gets everyone thinking about what can be done differently next time to avoid mistakes and sets the stage for the innovation of new and better products and processes.[8] What is just as important as understanding what has worked is understanding what didn't work, so it doesn't happen again.

Mistakes are inevitable. A common mistake I make at Gopuff is bringing on new items that I think will be successful but don't end up selling. In fact, about 30% of items brought on end up not selling despite our best efforts. While it is expected that not every item will sell, don't assume these types of misses are unavoidable and insignificant. Instead, use all failures, even small ones, as learning opportunities.[9] Collaborate with your team about what went wrong, how to remedy the error, and what can be done differently next time.

You will never be 100% mistake-free, and no retailer will have

100% of their items sell. However, we should constantly strive for improvement. If 30% of our items are selling below expectations, let's set a goal and try to get that rate down to 25%. It is important to recognize when something is not working and be open to making changes.

For example, with underperforming items, I like to take the advice of Gopuff's cofounders, Rafael Ilishayev and Yakir Gola, who are proponents of "failing fast."* They assert that if something is not working, chances are it's not going to miraculously get better after two or three weeks. Instead of letting something continue to fail, fix it, and fix it fast. At Gopuff, that fix often means cutting our losses and taking an item off our shelves. Don't draw out or intensify a failure by sweeping it under the rug. Instead, acknowledge a mistake and give yourself or others an opportunity to provide a fix and improve the situation.

Failure is an inevitable and essential part of growth. Sharing failures leads to employee and company growth because it gets people thinking about what can be done differently and better next time. When you make a mistake, admit to it, take responsibility for your part, and figure out how to improve the situation.

HOW TO SHARE

Since becoming a manager, I regularly have asked team members during weekly team meetings to share a best practice or win from the week. This has allowed team members to receive individual recognition, learn from one another, and celebrate wins as a team

---

*For a discussion on failing fast, see Bryan Casey, "Failing Fast, Traditional Strategy, and How They Work Together," IBM: Cloud, October 4, 2019, https://www.ibm.com/cloud/blog/failing-fast-traditional-strategy-and-how-they-work-together.

(which goes a long way in strengthening team morale). In recent years, I have shaken things up and started asking my team to also share a mistake they made over the past week.

When I first asked about "failures," I got nothing but crickets. My team members were caught off guard. They were ready to share wins and brag to me and the team about what they had accomplished. However, no one seemed eager to share a failure.

So, I broke the ice and shared a failure I experienced during the week. This eased tensions and demonstrated that I value sharing mistakes. We now celebrate both failures and wins on my weekly team calls. I particularly appreciate hearing about the failures because they provide opportunities for us to truly learn from each other's experiences.

If your boss does not carve out a specific time for sharing mistakes (and I'm guessing most don't), that's okay. Mistakes can be shared with your boss or team at other strategic times.

Here are two of the best times to share your failures.

- **During a performance review with your boss. Be open about a failure.** Explain how you learned from the experience and are now less likely to repeat that kind of mistake. This disclosure can also help build trust between you and your boss.

- **During a team meeting. Be vulnerable and share an experience involving a failure.** You will stand out as a team leader by modeling learning from your mistakes, which is a best practice within the business industry.

Whether you're sharing with just your boss or the whole team, before sharing, figure out a plan (or at least a potential plan) to fix the error. This is much better than sharing a mistake and expecting others to come up with a solution or fix it. When you fix your own mistakes, you save others time and demonstrate accountability and growth from experience.

Can you talk about your failures too much? Yes. If you publicize that you've made the same type of failure repeatedly, you may appear incompetent. People could wonder, "How can you keep making that same mistake? Don't you learn from your mistakes?" When publicizing failures, frame them as learning experiences and teach the team what went wrong and what you will do differently next time.

Unfortunately, not every work team offers a supportive environment in which to share and learn from mistakes. Within these negative work cultures, employees do not trust others on their team have their best interests in mind, and they do not feel safe disclosing their own errors. This is a shame because research indicates that when workers are given the space and support to freely admit their errors, the entire team and organization benefits.[10]

If you find your team to be unsupportive and believe that sharing a mistake is too high-risk, at a minimum, acknowledge the mistake to yourself. Then, try to find and implement a fix, even if you won't be sharing it with others. (If you don't acknowledge something is not working, it won't get fixed and may worsen over time.)

Moreover, if you find yourself within a toxic work culture, consider taking a new job on a different team or with a new company altogether. In addition to negative mental health ramifications, a negative work culture can stunt your career growth, as these teams have lower performance and higher turnover rates, which ultimately weakens the entire company.[11] You might as well get off the ship before it starts sinking. (See the section Be Open to Climbing a New Ladder.)

What if you have a supportive work environment, but no one shares their failures? Does that mean you're the only one making mistakes? No—of course not! Everyone makes mistakes. It's possible that those who don't talk about theirs are nervous, scared, or insecure. Or they haven't read this book.

Be the better coworker and be the first to let others know you messed up, how it happened, and what you've done to fix it. If you're having trouble thinking of a potential solution, try problem-solving with a team member. When you admit your mistakes, you convey to your team members that they are sources of support rather than competition and that you all are working together toward shared goals. When you admit your failures, you can help your team become even more supportive and even more successful.

Share your mistake and how you've learned from it to strengthen your team and demonstrate personal growth. When you demonstrate that you can recognize and learn from mistakes, you show that you are ready to be promoted.

EXCUSES, EXCUSES

An important part of learning from your failures is recognizing how you contributed to an error. However, all too often, instead of taking responsibility, problems are met with excuses that begin with "It's not my fault . . .". Most likely, and especially when you're part of a team, nothing is 100% your fault. However, when your explanation for a mistake doesn't include some personal responsibility, what I end up hearing is "It's not my fault. I'm not to blame." If you are the project owner and there is an issue, take responsibility.

When an explanation for a problem or error doesn't include any personal responsibility, it is generally considered a poor excuse. The following are poor excuses that end up making you look bad:

- **"I don't know because they didn't get back to me."** I get frustrated just writing this one down. If you need an answer and someone didn't respond to your *one* email, which may have gotten lost among the hundreds your recipient got that day, then pick up the phone and call. If they don't return your call, call again. You get the picture. (See the Know When Email Is Not Enough section.)

- **"I don't have the resources/time/manpower to get that done."** We are all overworked and have too many projects to complete within the given hours in a day. Complaining you have too much work annoys me and probably annoys others. Don't say it without providing a solution. Give me a way to fix the situation. If someone tells me what help they need, I can usually figure out how to make sure they get it. (See the Make Your Own Meetings section.)

- **"My computer doesn't work"** or **"I can't get on the Internet."** Okay, what did you do to resolve this issue? Have you talked to IT? If IT is not getting back to you, have you asked your manager to reach out to IT on your behalf? Do not just sit back and wait. Instead, be assertive and proactive and get technical problems fixed ASAP.

Excuses like these paralyze you from solving a problem because they attribute the problem to factors outside of your control. Instead of trying to spin it so you are not to blame, when things don't go the way you want, just own it. Once you can realize your role in creating or maintaining a problem, you will be better suited to fix the problem and prevent it from happening again.[12]

The worst thing you can do to avoid taking responsibility is to lie. Don't lie. It is unacceptable and could get you fired. I have seen a lie turn a relatively minor situation into one with significant negative consequences.

I remember sitting in my boss's office when he called one of his key account managers.

"Are you at your desk?" my boss asked.

"Yes. I'm here," the key account manager replied.

"What are you working on?" my boss casually asked.

"A sales presentation for a meeting with my Buyer later today," he answered.

"I am about to go into a meeting," my boss said. "Can you send me that report you showed me the other day on Texas performance?"

"Uh . . . well, I'm actually getting my hair cut right now."

This little lie, which didn't even involve me (I only happened to be in the office), has forever soured my impression of this person. Every time I talk to this guy now, I think about how he lied about getting a haircut. It makes me wonder what else he is lying about and whether he is lying to me. In many jobs (such as his), it's okay to be away from your computer to run a quick errand. It is unfortunate that such an unnecessary lie tainted my and likely my boss's impression of him.

Lying can be a slippery slope. Instead of risking sliding down that hill, make a habit of being truthful. Be straightforward and candid if you are unsure about something. If someone asks you for a specific number and you don't know the answer, say something like "I think it's *x*, but let me double-check." If you find out something you said was incorrect, notify the person you told right away.

Lies will eventually come back to bite you in the butt. When they do, relationships will be damaged. Once someone catches you lying, even if not to them directly, you will likely lose that person's trust forever. Don't jeopardize losing others' respect and possibly your job over an unnecessary lie. Instead of making an excuse or telling a lie, admit your mistakes.

It will be difficult to grow within your company if you don't acknowledge your mistakes and recognize how you contributed to an error. When you fail at something (and remember, we all will have many failures), acknowledge the failure, figure out what went wrong, and have the courage to share your failure with your team. That way, everyone has the opportunity to learn from your mistake.

When you let go of the mindset that others are the source of your problems, you empower yourself to act and find solutions. Instead of hiding your mistakes, admit to them, learn from them, and grow from them. You will ultimately become a better team member and stronger employee.

BE A TEAM LEADER

For teams to succeed, they need people who are willing—and even eager—to be team leaders. Team leaders provide essential support to not only their teammates but also to their bosses, who need people to step up and help things get accomplished. When a boss is looking to promote someone on their team, their first pick will likely be a person who is already a team leader. Two ways to demonstrate that you are a team leader are volunteering to lead projects and taking on more responsibility.

LEAD PROJECTS

When your boss is looking for someone to lead a project, you may think it's in your best interest to keep quiet. Why give yourself more work and risk making mistakes with unfamiliar tasks if someone else will inevitably take care of it? I'll tell you why: to get promoted and not be stagnant in your career, you need to step up. You need to do more than just meet the minimum job expectations (even if you are doing so flawlessly). You need to exceed expectations and do extra things like volunteer to lead projects.

In team meetings, I commonly propose projects that need to be started. I typically bring them up to the whole group instead of one individual, so if a particular project speaks to someone on my team, they have the opportunity to speak up and take the lead. By not assigning the project to a specific person, I open the door for anyone on the team to step up. If no one steps up, nothing gets done.

You don't need to step up every time. I wouldn't expect someone to say "yes" every single time, nor would I want that. If I have a team of five people and propose one project a week for five weeks, I expect everyone to take on at least one of those projects. If you don't, then you're not meeting my expectations. If you want to exceed expectations, you should take on more than one project.

Volunteering to lead a project doesn't mean volunteering to do all the work. A project's leader can bring on other team members and seek out cross-functional support for assistance. Also, a project can have two leads who share responsibility.

An important part of being a manager is being able to successfully lead projects. When you lead a project, you demonstrate an ability to delegate and keep multiple contributors organized and on schedule. In this respect, when you lead projects, you show that you can handle more senior roles.

I had an employee, Mike, who was a natural team leader. When he led a project, he took the initiative to create a Gannt chart. The chart summarized a project's different components, when each component was due, and the people heading each component.*

When Mike and I would meet during his weekly one-on-one meeting, he reviewed the Gannt chart by going over what's been completed, what's left to do, and problematic issues that could arise. He was, to say the least, very diligent about keeping track of where he was in the process. This diligence served him well. Knowing how thorough he was, I often asked him to lead future projects. Mike was promoted multiple times within the team over the period of just a few years.

You don't need to wait until your boss is "asking for volunteers" to step up and lead a project. If you're on the lookout and willing to challenge yourself, you will likely find a lot of opportunities to step up, help your team, and be a team leader.

STEP IN AS A SUBSTITUTE

Stepping up isn't only about leading projects. You can also be a team leader by jumping in and assuming responsibility when there is a

---

*A Gantt chart, developed by Henry Gantt, is a popular project-management tool to track projects and their due dates. The chart provides a visual representation of a project's individual steps and their progress in relation to one another. "What Is a Gantt Chart?," Gantt.com, accessed July 9, 2022, https://www.gantt.com.

gap in leadership. Taking charge during times of transition provides you with an opportunity to help your team succeed while simultaneously showcasing your capabilities and advancing your career.

Periods of transition are often stressful for an organization. It often takes some time for duties to be reallocated and positions to be filled. Use these periods of transition as opportunities to step up. For example, there may be a time when your immediate supervisor's position opens if they leave the company or get promoted. Take the initiative to step up and cover their responsibilities, even if nobody asks you to. This may entail completing reports for management, providing direction to peers, or answering customers' questions.

One of my colleagues was working at a beer distributor when his boss abruptly left. No one had been assigned his boss's tasks, such as attending to daily service calls that needed to be scheduled and split among the sales reps. He took it upon himself to assume these responsibilities on top of his regular job of opening new accounts. After a week, he let the Branch Sales Manager know what he had been doing. This ultimately led to his promotion within the company a few months later.

Even if this kind of opportunity doesn't present itself, find opportunities to step up and take on responsibilities that otherwise would fall through the cracks. You certainly don't need to wait until something is asked of or assigned to you to take on extra responsibilities.

Team leaders show eagerness and initiative. Team leaders volunteer more than is expected and even before they're asked. Team leaders step up—and team leaders get promoted.

RECAP

When you want to get promoted, instead of focusing on helping yourself, put energy into helping your team. Here's how:

- Use "we" instead of "I" at work. This illustrates your dedication to your team and your team members' shared goals.

- Be positive. Monitor your words and body language to make sure you're not giving off negative vibes. A boss wants to be around and will promote people who are positive.

- Add value. Speak up when you're in a meeting, and don't be afraid to disagree with your boss and team members.

- Ask for help. When you don't ask, you risk doing things incorrectly and can end up giving your boss more work instead of less.

- Admit your mistakes. Instead of making an excuse, acknowledge what went wrong and find a way to make it right. Mistakes can be learning opportunities for everyone on the team when you examine what went wrong and figure out what to do differently next time.

- Be a team leader. Step up to lead projects and assume responsibility whenever you can to showcase your talents, drive, and enthusiasm.

Working well within a team is a crucial part of succeeding in the workforce. When you prioritize supporting your team and working with them toward shared goals, you help yourself and your career.

PART 2

GOING ABOVE AND BEYOND

TWO OF MY DIRECT REPORTS, Tyler and Brandon, were in a meeting with my boss (aka their boss's boss). The meeting was open-ended, without an agenda, and they could talk to my boss about whatever they wanted. Tyler presented a PowerPoint presentation on why beer out-of-stocks (OOS) were rising and a strategy to sell single-serve beers that could grow revenue and margins. Brandon, on the other hand, didn't present anything or have any specific questions.

Their difference in actions was not a one-off. Instead, it was a snapshot of why Tyler was a star employee on track to be promoted and Brandon was not. Tyler didn't just show up at the meeting and do the minimum. Instead, he went above and beyond.

We could all get through our workday, do what needs to be done, and come back the next day and do it all over again. However, to move (way) up in a company, you must do more than the minimum. Executing your job's day-to-day tasks and responsibilities is essential, but it's not enough.

To avoid stagnation in your position, you need to demonstrate that you can anticipate the next question, identify problems, think outside the box, find answers, and implement initiatives. You don't want to just come up with ideas; you want your ideas to be adopted and implemented with success. Then, in your next interview, when you are asked, "What did you do in your last role to improve your company?" you can blow them away with your answer.

Part 2, Going Above and Beyond, challenges you to step out from behind your day-to-day duties and demonstrate that you can handle more. Going Above and Beyond provides a step-by-step guide on how to identify problems and implement solutions, provide data-driven answers to questions, and produce powerful presentations so you can get the YES. This section concludes with strategic steps you can take now that can set you up for long-term career success.

If you're not interested in going above and beyond, you can skip this section and call it a day. However, if you are driven and motivated to go the distance, keep reading. I'll teach you even more secrets to becoming a person who gets promoted.

CHAPTER 6

CREATE BEST PRACTICES

TO GET PROMOTED INTO senior roles within a company, you need to do more than just execute tasks. Senior positions are for those who can identify ways to improve the company and bring those ideas to fruition. In other words, the employees who are promoted are the employees who create best practices.

In the business industry, the term "best practice" describes a business practice known to produce optimal results. I use the term best practice to describe any new project or procedure implemented that saves the company resources (i.e., time, money), decreases mistakes or defects, or improves production or service. In essence, "best practice" is an elevated (or fancy) way to describe a new way of doing something that helps everything run smoother.

You probably have already created a best practice, even if you didn't call it that. So, when speaking to your boss or other senior employees, don't be afraid to use the term "best practice" to describe projects you created or helped with that led to improvements in your company.

My first job after college was with the market research company IRI. I was on the Anheuser-Busch account and worked at A-B's Midwest Region office in Chicago. My regular job responsibilities included updating weekly sales reports for the beer category, answering specific requests using deep-dive analyses, and finding opportunities to grow A-B sales within my region. I did those tasks, but I also went above and beyond by creating a monthly newsletter for the 100 A-B employees in my office. The newsletter contained the latest sales and industry news for the beer category (as well as some fun facts). Each month for about a year, I put a hard copy on everyone's desk or mailed it to them. I received feedback from many that it was very helpful to see the most important information all in one place.

No one told me to create this. I did it proactively to get my coworkers to read and review beer sales. This type of project could be described as a "best practice" and should certainly be highlighted during a performance evaluation or job interview. After all, businesses want and recognize employees who create best practices.

Anheuser-Busch has best practice competitions to encourage and reward employees who develop best practices. To help their employees create strong best practices, A-B sponsors Six Sigma training programs.* I participated in A-B's Six Sigma Green Belt and Six Sigma Black Belt programs and strongly recommend taking advantage of these training opportunities if they're available within your company.

One best practice I created through the Six Sigma program was an app to decrease A-B out-of-stocks in Walmart.** Once completed, the app helped reduce those stores' out-of-stocks by 25%.

Not all best practices need to be as complex as developing an app. A best practice could be as simple as creating an Excel

---

*Information about Six Sigma can be found at https://www.6sigma.us/.

**Out-of-stock is when a retailer runs out of a product(s) being sold on their shelves. When items are out-of-stock, you run the risk of losing sales and upsetting your consumers.

report that integrates information from four separate reports or implementing a weekly conference call with another department to facilitate cross-functional communication.

When I was VP of Walmart Sales for Anheuser-Busch, one of my direct reports implemented a twice-monthly call between our Walmart Sales team and the A-B Supply and Logistics team. The purpose of the call was for our Sales team to increase communication with the Supply and Logistics team about newly approved SKUs and programs (i.e., promotions and displays) going into Walmart. The Supply and Logistics team needed to be the first to know when we sold a new item into Walmart so they could ensure the breweries were able to produce the product and meet the agreed-upon timelines.

Prior to the biweekly call, inconsistent communication between the two departments contributed to issues with product supply. This new call enabled more precise production planning and minimized out-of-stocks by streamlining communication between the two departments.

Identifying problems or areas of weakness is the first step in creating a great best practice.

IMAGINE IMPROVEMENT

The hardest part of creating a best practice can sometimes be figuring out what to create. If something is such a good idea, why hasn't someone already thought of it? In Daniel H. Pink's *Masterclass*, Pink highlights the importance of "problem-finders" over problem-solvers. He explained that problem-finders discover solutions to problems people didn't realize that they had.[1] To develop a great best practice, we often need to become problem-finders and find those problems others didn't even know existed.

Finding a problem to solve is not always easy. Once we grow accustomed to doing something a certain way, we become blind to the fact that it is inefficient, redundant, or doesn't make sense. The longer we've been doing it, the harder it is to see that there is a better way.

To become a better problem-finder, keep a running list of ideas for best practices. Throughout your day, jot down processes that seem inefficient and ideas for improving them. I find this practice to be particularly worthwhile when beginning a new role. Then, when you are ready to start making changes, return to this list for inspiration.

I recommend working hard to come up with best practices early in your career. This will give you the reputation of being a "self-starter" (which is how I describe employees who come up with their own best practices). Self-starters are the type of employee bosses like to promote.

You don't need to think of ideas for best practices all on your own. In many companies, managers bring up projects that need spearheading to their teams (as discussed in Be a Team Leader). Jump onboard these best practices. Projects specifically requested by your boss are the projects most likely to be approved for cross-functional support, financial support, and implementation. It's smart to join these best practices that will likely make it to the finish line.

A best practice is more than just a great idea. Imagining innovation is just the first step in developing a best practice. For a best practice to be achieved, it needs to progress from the drawing board. For that to happen, there needs to be collaboration.

COLLABORATE WITH COLLEAGUES

Don't work in a bubble and surprise everyone at the last minute with a project. When creating a best practice, collaborate with colleagues in order to receive feedback, secure resources, and facilitate buy-in.

Feedback is key to a best practice's success. If you implement a project without any feedback from anyone, I would be concerned. The creator of a best practice is inherently biased. Using someone else's eyes to reexamine the idea can help your best practice become even better.

You want feedback from the people who will be using and benefiting from the best practice. Don't just talk to them once. Keep them apprised of your progress, and be open to their feedback and suggestions along the way. Your users will be more likely to take on your best practice if they have a say in its creation. The more feedback you get, the more likely others will actually use it once complete.

A best practice is something that benefits your company. In that respect, don't be afraid to reach out to other departments for help. Cross-functional support is often necessary to secure the resources you need. If you are working on a technical project, you might need help from the IT team. If you are working on a sales project, you might need data from multiple sales teams. Take advantage of the resources (whether manpower, time, or money) available within your company to make your best practice a success.

Finding money to complete a project can be challenging. Many best practices, such as bringing on new software or partnering with IRI to buy data, will cost money. I recommend putting together a return on investment (ROI) analysis. (Some companies have existing ROI templates.) An ROI outlines the cost of a project, how long it will take to recoup the money, and how long it will take to make a profit. Talk to your boss about who would be the best person to present the ROI to. If you have an expensive project, such as one that adds new employees or positions and costs over $100,000 per person, it's usually best to start small. When possible, develop a pilot program to show sustainable results, before asking for a lot more money.

As you collaborate, it is natural for colleagues to become increasingly invested in your best practice's development and eventual implementation. When collaborators believe in your cause, they will be more likely to approve financing, provide resources, or comply with implementation. In other words, the more you collaborate, the more "buy-in" you will get. Don't create a best practice and then try to get buy-in at the end. Instead, get buy-in throughout the development of a best practice as you collaborate.

A great time to get buy-in is when presenting about your best practice. During your presentation, emphasize how your best practice will save time and money. The goal isn't for people to just recognize it's a good idea, but to be so swayed that they invest themselves in helping make it a success. (See the chapters Get the Yes and Present Like a Pro for information about presentations and how to get others to say "yes" to your requests.)

Getting support from people within and outside of your team is an important part of creating a successful best practice. Collaboration is essential for developing a best practice and ensuring it is implemented and maintained over time.

GO THE DISTANCE

Best practices take time. That's time to create, time to develop, and—once you think you might be done—more time to ensure implementation at the onset and in the future.

Best practices require putting in time beyond what you spend on your day-to-day tasks. Some best practices, like organizing a cross-functional meeting, could be designed and implemented within a matter of hours. Other best practices take weeks or months to develop. The app used to reduce out-of-stocks took six months to complete.

Whether your best practice is a relatively simple or an elaborate endeavor, make sure you are disciplined enough to complete the task. Time and time again, I have seen coworkers begin best practices only to get distracted by ad hoc projects and end up never finishing their best practice.

If you come to a stalemate after getting stuck or losing motivation, don't risk abandoning a potential great best practice. Instead, do what you can to get back on track. Try collaborating with others. You could find someone else to co-lead the project with you. When you work with others, you can hold each other accountable. You could also try presenting your progress. The preparation for the presentation and the feedback you receive can give you new insight and energize you to keep going. If you happen to be promoted before finishing the project, make sure you transition your best practice to your replacement.

Once your best practice is complete, you will likely need to invest more time into making revisions and ensuring implementation.

Just like an app goes through multiple iterations with new versions regularly released to fix glitches, you may need to release multiple versions of your best practice. You may find glitches when you initially present it to your team or when people start using it. Later on down the line, changes in other processes may lead to your best practice needing to be updated. A best practice often has to be continually maintained, so it doesn't become obsolete. If someone is not actively fixing bugs, the best practice will become inefficient and eventually stop being used. Best practices almost always need, often unexpected, fixes and adjustments.

Our Gopuff Beverage team developed a best practice to speed up the process of adding and removing items. An eight-week trial period was created for all new items. After the eight-week test phase, we would determine whether an item's sales were strong enough to remain on our platform. If the item wasn't selling well, we decided we would rather they "fail fast" so it could be removed and replaced with another item.

To determine whether new items were a success during their trial periods, we needed an efficient way to analyze the sales data. Specifically, we needed a report to compare each new item's sales to a unique criterion based on the sales within that item's subcategory (e.g., hard seltzer, craft, etc.) and particular test market(s). If a product met the criterion, it would indicate we reached enough sales to continue selling the item on the platform.

I tasked a new employee on our team, Sang, with creating the best practice. I had heard from his line manager that he was very strong in Excel and believed he had the skills to spearhead this project. He took about one week to create a template in Excel and then set up a meeting with the team to review it and train them on how to run the sales report.

During the presentation, Sang noticed a few errors in his formulas. Also, after he presented, I requested that the report be edited so it could easily be forwarded to suppliers without the extra sheets containing formula instructions and raw data. Within twenty-four hours, Sang re-sent the final report to the team. When developing a best practice, anticipate that there will be bugs or errors that need fixing. Be prepared to make timely corrections to ensure the best practice can be implemented and utilized.

Getting people to use your best practice should also be a priority. At first, many new best practices have strong utilization but see less engagement over time. Employees need to be reminded to use new processes, as people often revert to what they're used to even after being shown a better way. If your boss mandates that your best practice be implemented, as was the case with our eight-week trial period, you're a step ahead. Still, mandatory implementation is not a substitute for getting buy-in through collaboration and feedback during development and implementation from the people who will be using it.

When creating a best practice, you need to go the distance. Be sure to complete it, fix it, and maintain it.

RECAP

When I interview a candidate for a position, I always ask what best practices they implemented in their past positions that saved time or money. Bosses and companies want people on their team and promote people who are problem-solvers, people who can identify a problem and create solutions. Prove you're one of these go-getters by creating and implementing best practices.

- Show your boss you can take the initiative and create something new.

- Figure out an approach that saves time or money for the company.

- When you begin a new role, keep a running list of procedures you believe need improving.

- Be prepared to devote time, ask for feedback, get support from your peers, secure funds, and get buy-in from your end-users for your best practice to succeed.

Think of how to make your job easier, and then make it happen. Don't just complacently do the day-to-day tasks of your position. Instead, be remembered as the person who implements projects that save time, make money, and wow the customer!

CHAPTER 7

SOLVE PROBLEMS SYSTEMATICALLY

WHETHER YOU'RE COMPLETING a best practice, answering a question posed by your boss, or tackling something for yourself, it is best to solve problems systematically. This chapter provides a framework for coming up with accurate, data-driven solutions to questions, communicating your findings, and avoiding unnecessary blunders along the way. Solving problems systematically necessitates that you clarify the question, decode the data, and share your solution.

CLARIFY THE QUESTION

Imagine you've just spent several days on a project. You ran numbers and created an in-depth slideshow with charts and projections. You present it to your boss, expecting she will be impressed, but instead, she looks puzzled and shakes her head.

"No," she says, "this isn't what I was asking for." Talk about feeling deflated! All that work—to answer the wrong question! The lesson of the story is this: always be sure you understand the assignment.

You can't give the correct answer if you are asking the wrong question. Make sure to clarify the question or assignment before getting started. Early in my career, I had to redo about 50% of my work due to misunderstanding the question. About 25% of the time, my bosses had either poorly communicated the question or did not fully understand the question themselves. (Admittedly, about 75% of the time, it was completely my fault.)

When asked a question or given an assignment, I recommend:

- writing down the question (if it is presented verbally),
- restating the referral question, and
- asking additional questions to make sure the question is perfectly clear.

Often, employees are hesitant to ask for clarification. As a manager, I would rather have someone clarify the question and do it right the first time than not clarify the question and do it incorrectly.

Clarifying the question, while seemingly simple, is potentially the most important step in Solve Problems Systematically. If you misunderstand the question or are not on the same page as those who need the answers, you will end up wasting time and probably frustrating others. Don't get too excited and rush into solving a problem by answering a question without first clarifying it.

DECODE THE DATA

"It must have been the weather." I hear this response far too often when there are questions about slumping sales. I hear "Sales are down because it rained" or "sales are down because the temperature was ten degrees colder than last year." You get the picture.

Weather is ever-changing. Yes, it might impact sales, but rarely does it explain 100% of the issue.

When your boss asks what contributed to decreased sales, don't just share speculative answers as if you're in the midst of an open-ended brainstorming session. Sure, we can all share a couple of ideas, but don't stop there.

Look at the data to figure out what really happened. It may seem like a mystery at first. But trust me, if you look closely enough at the data, you will likely find the real answer to your question. Maybe you lacked displays or ads in comparison to last year. Maybe the competition did something bigger, which disrupted your performance. Decode the data to find the answer.

It is important to understand what data you have access to. Often, employees are unaware of available data, essentially at their fingertips. To better understand your data options, talk to a veteran member of your team or someone on the data analytics team, who can often help you figure out the kind of data available and how to access it.

Sometimes, the data you need is in an existing report and ready to interpret. Other times, you will need to input raw data into software (like Excel) to analyze. From there, you can interpret and draw conclusions from the data.

In addition, to looking at your company's data, don't forget to utilize other data too. For example, you can access *competitive data*, such as the retail price of similar competitive items at other retailers, by looking on the Internet. Or you can use census data to understand the demographics of a market. I consider this type of data *consumer insights data*. (See the following example for information on types of data typically used in Sales.)

DECODING DATA IN SALES

The three types of data I use most often to decode data in Sales are: point-of-sale data, competitive data, and consumer insights data.

Point-of-sale data is internal data that typically only employees from your company have access to. It includes specific items' revenue, units sold, cost, retail price, etc. Many companies will have an internal portal where you log in and pull the data you need. You may be able to access previously created reports or create your own reports by identifying and analyzing specific metrics.

Competitive data allows companies to compare their sales to their competitors. You could find some competitive data on your own by looking at other stores' assortments or retail prices through online or in-store market visits. The most valuable competitive data is competitors' sales data. Most companies will only have access to this type of data through third-party businesses, such as IRI or Nielsen, which sell competitive data to retailers and suppliers.

Consumer insights data shows who and why someone buys a product. This type of data can be very important when deciding which product to sell and how to market to the right audience. Consumer insights data could come from a third-party or be derived from surveys and focus groups conducted by your company. My favorite consumer insights metric is *repeat rate*. Repeat rate is the percentage of customers who buy an item two or more times within a select period of time. (It's easy to get a consumer to buy your item once, but you really want your consumer to buy your item again and again.)

As you gather data, it is important to keep it organized. This is especially important if your project extends over a long period and you need to return to the data later, for edits or more analyses. Organized information also allows for others (e.g., colleagues, bosses) to easily review all steps of your analyses.

If you are working in Excel, save all your data in one workbook with tabs (or sheets) for different data pulls and reports. It is much easier to review one Excel workbook than to be forced to look in multiple workbooks that can end up in different places within your computer.

Let's look at an example of when I decoded data to solve a problem.

I had been at Gopuff for about a year when my boss emailed our team, congratulating us on the Alcohol category's strong performance last week. Alcohol showed huge growth compared to all other categories on our platform (Snacks, Ice Cream, Home Essentials, etc.). Both our sales and our margin had grown. It seemed too good to be true. My boss asked me, "What's behind the huge growth?" I had a question that needed an answer.

The change seemed too large to be accounted for by random fluctuations in sales. I started to brainstorm explanations for the upswing. I knew we hadn't run any substantial promotions or significantly changed pricing. I couldn't come up with a clear hypothesis for the growth. So, I just started exploring the data to look for answers.

First, I tried to determine which kind of alcohol (i.e., beer, wine, spirits) grew the most. I found that sales and margins for each type of alcohol grew at roughly the same rate. I then looked at subclass data (i.e., craft beer, white wine, whiskey, etc.)—still nothing. So, I looked at brands and individual SKUs. No matter how specific I got, I saw similar performance across the board. I couldn't find anything to help me understand the dramatic increase in sales. I was thoroughly perplexed.

I finally looked at orders containing alcohol that used discount (coupon) codes. I noticed the "discount dollars" over the past week were basically $0, which meant no one had used a discount code towards their alcohol purchase.

Then it hit me! Last week, the company implemented a change, and discount codes could no longer be applied toward the purchase of alcohol. This resulted in our margins skyrocketing because, in essence, we were making more profit on alcohol than we did last week. (The data also demonstrated that we could maintain strong alcohol sales without coupon codes.) I was then able to provide my boss with a logical, data-supported explanation for the unexpected growth. The answer to the question about the unexpected rise in alcohol sales was clear cut. It was only a matter of me figuring it out.

Often, there is not one clear-cut answer to a question. For better or for worse, it is usually possible to create multiple compelling, data-supported answers. Data can be interpreted in different ways. Many questions have different "correct" answers, depending on which data was examined and how it was analyzed and interpreted. Moreover, there may be an infinite number of variables that potentially contribute to a situation and that can be examined.

The more data you decode, the more informative, nuanced, and accurate your answer will likely be. However, even the most driven employees can get sidetracked exploring data, especially because more information often leads to more questions. At some point, you need to stop digging for data and come up with what you think is the best and most accurate answer to the original question. Finding correct answers will set the stage for a strong presentation of your findings.

SHARE YOUR SOLUTION

Now that you have clarified the question and decoded the data, it's time to share your solution. When sharing your solution, it is imperative that you answer the question. It's easy to get sidetracked with interesting information you discovered and want to share. However, you may soon realize that you never shared the answer to the question (or never found the answer in the first place).

When sharing your solution, you must stay on track and communicate the most important information as effectively as possible. While the section Present Like a Pro will provide a more in-depth discussion about presenting to an audience, the following recommendations are important to consider when sharing your solution:

- Start off by rephrasing the referral question. It is important to remind your audience what was originally asked.

- Identify the data sources used to answer the question. (You do not need to show the raw data.)

- Focus the presentation on the most critical and pertinent information.

- Communicate the information in multiple ways. Not everyone learns the same. Some people, like myself, process information best when numbers are used. Others prefer information to be explained with words; some prefer to hear the information; others prefer to see the information. You can always ask the person to whom you are presenting how they prefer to have the findings delivered.

- If applicable, provide recommendations or next steps. These should be simple, concise (potentially bullet-pointed) ideas on what you think the best course of action should be.

- Prepare for follow-up questions. Supplemental information can be added to an appendix or presented when applicable questions are asked.

Sharing your solution is essential to solving problems systematically. If you do great work but do not present your solution well, you did not do great work. The better you clarify the question and decode data, the easier it will be to effectively share your solution.

RECAP

To go above and beyond, you should solve problems systematically. While this is not necessarily a linear process, there are three steps to keep in mind:

- Clarify the question to be answered. There's no point wasting time on answering the wrong question.

- Decode the data. Take time to find, analyze, and interpret pertinent data.

- Share your solution. Be thorough, support your answers with data, and anticipate new questions.

When you use data to solve problems, you demonstrate that people can depend on you to provide accurate, credible answers. You demonstrate that you are ready to be promoted.

CHAPTER 8

GET THE YES

REGARDLESS OF YOUR SPECIFIC JOB or what company you work for, you are likely trying to influence people one way or another.* Whether you're attempting to pitch a new idea, secure funding for a best practice, or sell your item into a retailer, you're in a situation where you're selling something, asking for something, or needing others to act. At the end of the day, you need your audience to agree to what you're proposing. You need to get the YES.

This chapter provides strategies to help you get the YES. These strategies include stating your request, using data to back up your request, and understanding what motivates your audience. This chapter further identifies how consistent and transparent follow-up strengthens your relationship with your client and helps you get the YES again and again.

MAKE THE ASK

I remember joining a meeting with Walmart's West Coast Beer Buyer to discuss A-B beer sales within their Western Region. A-B

---

*For an interesting discussion on this, see Daniel H. Pink, *To Sell Is Human: The Surprising Truth about Moving Others* (New York: Riverhead, 2012).

was underperforming in that region, and we needed to develop a plan for how to get our sales back on track. My boss happened to be in town, so he joined the meeting too.

Our Sales Director (my direct report) led the meeting, as it was his scheduled monthly meeting. My boss and I were just sitting in. The Sales Director gave a "here's what we're doing" presentation. I could tell he thought the meeting was going well. However, my boss and I noticed a big problem. He never asked for anything. At the end, the Buyer even looked at him and asked, "Anything else?"

The Sales Director shook his head. "No. I'm good."

My boss looked at me in complete disbelief and frustration. The Sales Director could have asked the Walmart Beer Buyer for any number of things to help grow our sales: more displays, a new product added to the shelves, another promotion—anything. The Buyer was pretty much inviting the Sales Director to "make an ask," but he never did. This meeting strained the relationship between my boss and this Sales Director.

When I was a supplier meeting with retailers, I might have asked for five to ten different things in a typical thirty-minute sales meeting. I may have asked the retailer to accept my product, display it, promote it, or give it more shelf space. Now that I'm a retailer meeting with suppliers, I ask for better marketing support, to be the first to market (the first retailer to sell their new item), or for money to support promotions. Making the ask will always be a priority, whatever my role.

People often feel uncomfortable making the ask. Maybe they don't want to be rejected or don't want to pressure others and make them feel uncomfortable. If you struggle with this, you can look at it another way. People often need direction and a push to make changes and improvements. Otherwise, they default to the status quo. When you present, this is your opportunity to tell your audience what actions they need to take to create change. By spelling out what they should do, you are helping them.

Making the ask is not just for external clients. You can use these same strategies when making internal requests, like when seeking buy-in for a best practice. Whether making an ask internally or externally, it is important to know who the decision-makers are. You don't want to waste time asking the wrong people or get a yes from people who aren't at liberty to make those decisions.

When making the ask, follow the company's hierarchy. You don't want to go to your boss's boss or your Buyer's boss without your direct contact's permission. (I have been guilty of this on multiple occasions, and it always reflected poorly on me.) If you do present above your boss, make sure your boss is fully in the loop about what is being presented.

Develop a clear vision of what you plan to ask for. Don't waste time or insult your audience by asking for things you know they will not agree to. Instead, be precise and strategic with your requests. If you are selling an expensive, high-end item, you could focus your efforts on getting distribution in high-income stores (a term used for stores in locations where the average customer has a higher income) rather than requesting full distribution in all their stores.

Once you know exactly what you would like to ask for, curate a presentation that identifies and supports your asks. Rank your requests, and present them in order of priority. Your most significant opportunities (the things that will drive the most sales or be most beneficial) should be first, followed by less important requests. After each ask, provide support for your ask. (See the Use Data to Persuade section.)

When you prepare and have data-supported information to back you up, you will be more influential when making your asks. Still, regardless of how influential I think I am, it is rare that all my requests are agreed to exactly as I ask them. There will usually be back and forth when making an ask. It can be helpful to plan in your head how the other side may respond and what you could say next. Be prepared to negotiate.

Negotiations can get frustrating, particularly when you feel squeezed between not meeting your goals and losing a customer. In these challenging situations, stay cool and continue to show respect to your customer. You are not a celebrity investor on Shark Tank. Don't be demeaning or rude. Refrain from insisting you know more than the other person. Take a "helper" approach instead of a "power-over" approach, which can push the other party farther away rather than bring you closer to an agreement.[1]

During difficult negotiations, communicate in a way that portrays a desire for *both* sides to win. Think of the other person as a collaborator and the two of you as "building something together and both being better off."[2] Over the years, I have tried to approach negotiations with a win-win mindset, maintain a positive attitude, and go above and beyond to satisfy the customer.

Negotiation is a hard skill. Many folks benefit from taking negotiation training courses, and it is common for some retailers to require their Buyers to take negotiation courses. There is always room for improvement when it comes to negotiation.*

When making the ask, you may not get an answer right away. Some Buyers don't say a word until the end of a presentation.

---

*The Gap Partnership, https://www.thegappartnership.com/us/, is one company that offers negotiation training.

For others, the meeting may be more of an interactive discussion where feedback is provided immediately after each request. (That's another reason it's important to present your asks in order of priority—in case you run out of time!) Still, others make no decisions in the meeting and get back to you a few days later. Accordingly, you should always be prepared to make an ask and negotiate, even outside of scheduled meetings.

As I have progressed in my career, I have learned not to be shy about asking for what I want from my company, my boss, my team, and my customer. In order to get the YES, you need to make the ask. Be straightforward, strategic, and prepared to negotiate when making the ask. Take a helper approach and be gracious—especially when you get the YES. If you have a captive audience, don't waste your chance. When you learn how to make the ask, you learn how to get what you want from your customer and from your career.

USE DATA TO PERSUADE

I regularly have meetings with suppliers who want Gopuff to sell their line of beverages. They usually tout how well their products are selling. It's not uncommon for me to engage in this type of exchange during a meeting:

Me: "Where are your top markets?"

Supplier: "I sell great in all the markets that I distribute in—LA, New York City, the Midwest, the Pacific Northwest. I'm killing it in Texas and Florida. I just launched in North and South Carolina, and we are crushing it there."

Me: "Which SKUs are selling well?"

Supplier: "All our SKUs are selling great. There are no duds."

I know it is very rare for a new item (and all its SKUs) to be killing it in nearly every single geographic region. The person doesn't show me any supporting sales data or any data comparing their sales to their competition. At this point, I'm turned off. I *am* persuaded, but not in the direction they want.

Now let's play out a meeting between a dream supplier and me.

Me: "Where are your top markets?"

Supplier: "I am distributed across the East Coast, but my best market is Charlotte, North Carolina. In Charlotte, we have the fastest-growing healthy energy drink, and I'm averaging seven units per store per week, which is twenty percent greater than the number two competitor."

At this point, the supplier shows me syndicated data on how their beverage performs against other beverages in the Charlotte market.

Me: "Which SKUs are selling well?"

Supplier: "The blueberry and raspberry are my top two SKUs and account for seventy percent of my total revenue. When compared to my other SKUs, they have the highest revenue and highest repeat rate."

These are the kind of data-supported responses I find persuasive and would get me to say YES.

Money is a driving force (or at least a contributing factor) in most business decisions. Accordingly, when applicable, financial data should be included when making an ask. Examples of financial data important to me as a retailer are:

- the product's cost,
- total dollar sales in the last fifty-two weeks,
- year-over-year trend, and

- estimated incremental opportunity rate (based on an item's differentiation; see Appendix 1).

Persuasive data doesn't always have to be numerical. Non-numerical data can include information about a competitor's product, the ingredients in your product, or expert or customer testimony. Any fact can be used as supportive data.

When I meet with suppliers who want their beverage to be sold on Gopuff, I may want the following types of non-quantitative data:

- Is the product sugar-free, gluten-free, or plant-based?
- How does it differ from similar beverages?
- What marketing initiatives are in place?
- Do you have influencers supporting your product?

Answering questions with both numerical and non-numerical data is an important step to getting the YES.

Success in selling comes from having data to back you up. Always, *always* use data to make your case. Saying, "This is going to work" or "Sell my item in your store" does not make for a powerful case. I have to see it to believe it.

A powerful case is made when you have data to support your ask and show how your product, idea, or plan benefits your audience.

KNOW *THEIR* BUSINESS

To get the YES, it is important to not only know your business but to know *their* business as well. When preparing for a meeting, we often become hyper-focused on ourselves, our business, or our project. But we fail to put that same amount of energy into understanding the customer, client, or audience. When making an ask, learn about your customer and adapt your approach to match their goals.

On too many occasions, I have been in a meeting with a supplier and realized that the supplier didn't even know what Gopuff is. I then end up spending a large portion of the meeting educating them on information they could have Googled ahead of time. If they don't even know what Gopuff is, I doubt they tailored their presentation to highlight how their product would be a good fit for our customers.

When trying to get the YES, it is important to not just focus on yourself. You need to focus on them. You need to understand their company's culture and consumers, the factors they prioritize when making decisions, and how their employees are incentivized. Rather than repeating the exact same presentation with every audience, tailor your presentation for your customer.

I recommend sending an email to the person with whom you are meeting a week ahead of time explaining that you are preparing a presentation and have a few questions to help tailor your presentation. For example, if you were a new energy drink company planning on meeting with a retailer, you could ask some of the following questions:

- Can you tell me more about your customer?
- What are your top-selling markets?
- What is your process for adding new items?
- What is your strategy for the energy drink category?

You may not get a response, but that's okay. You should still try to do your own research. If you're friends with any other suppliers who work with that retailer, talk to them. Read industry news about the retailer. Search for their digital promotions. Go on the company's website or visit their store to get a feel for their brand. Don't go into a meeting blind about who you are selling to.

Another question you could ask is "How can I help you achieve your bonus?"

Understanding their KPIs or how your decision-maker is incentivized can help you tailor your presentation or pricing to be more in line with their goals.* (See Appendix 2 for more information about understanding your decision-maker's KPI.)

When communicating with your client, don't stick to using your company's internal language. Rather, mimic *their* corporate language.[3] You are on their turf, and you're trying to win them over. If they call their stores "clubs," you call them clubs, too. If they call their customers "guests," you do the same.

Instead of focusing only on *your* business, do research on *their* business. Understand their culture and their goals. Then, use data to explain how your product will help them reach their goals.

PLAN THE POST-GAME

After getting the YES (or even if you didn't), it's important to start thinking about your post-game. What can you do to reassure them they made the right decision? How can you get them to say YES again and again?

A strong post-game involves following up with accurate

---

*Key Performance Indicators (KPIs) are company goals presented quantitatively. The amount of an employee's bonus is often partially determined by how well they met their KPIs.

and timely data-informed feedback. I recommend scheduling a follow-up meeting immediately after getting the YES for one to four weeks later. During a follow-up meeting, results should always be shared—no matter what. Even if they are bad, it is important to show the other person that you understand where your gaps are and how you plan to fix them. Your number one objective is for your audience to have confidence you understand areas of weakness and can make them better.

When giving feedback, share your progress as it relates to goals. Goals can be created on your own or together with your client. When creating goals, identify the variable(s) that need to be tracked to monitor each goal's progress.

- If you're in *Sales*, your goal could be to grow sales by 10%. The variable you would track would be units sold.

- If you're in *Marketing*, your goal could be to increase social media engagement by 50%. You could track social media followers and impressions.

- If you're in *Operations*, your goal may be to reduce your out-of-stock rate from 7.5% to 6.8%. You could track inventory through retailer out-of-stock reports.

I recommend completing *action plans* to record your goals and monitor progress. An action plan (or action log) is a systematic way of keeping track of progress toward your goals.

I have seen many different action plans over the years. There is no one right template for it. Instead, action plans can be created and adapted to fit your needs. A good action plan might include the following components:

- The goal or target.

- Current results.

- The performance gap, which is the difference between the current results and your goal. (For example, if my goal was to sell 110 units, but I only sold fifty, the performance gap would be sixty units.)

- The action you plan to take to close each gap. There could be multiple actions per gap.

- The expected increase in units as a result of the action. Depending on the metric, you may be looking at dollars, share of category, etc.

- The person accountable for leading the action(s).

- The due date of the action.

- The status of your action (e.g., not started, in progress, complete).

- Any relevant notes.

Here is what an action plan at a beverage company may look like.

Objective	Current Results	Gap	Planned Action	Expected Change	Lead	Due	Status
Increase energy drink sales by 25%	+19%	-6%	1) Launch 50 new SKUs 2) Feature energy drinks on endcaps 3) Run 4 weeks of BOGO promotions	+37.5%	Tyler C.	1-Jun	In Progress
Increase Ready to Drink (RTD) Tequila assortment to 15 SKUs	10 SKUs	-5 SKUs	1) Look at IRI data to identify top RTD Tequila beverages 2) Meet with suppliers of brands we do not carry to discuss distribution opportunities 3) Launch 5 new RTD Tequila SKUs	+5 SKUs	Jane L.	1-Jun	Complete
Deliver $500k in sales with a beer and pizza cross-promotion	$0	$500k	1) Present program to our pizza and beer suppliers 2) Choose brands to participate in the promotion 3) Feature beer + pizza bundle in weekly emails	+$500	Noah T.	15-Jun	In Progress

I recommend creating an action plan during the meeting with your client, rather than after the fact. Since people sometimes come away from a meeting with different perceptions of how things will move forward, creating an action plan in real-time helps clarify discrepancies and ensures that all members' expectations are aligned. My former A-B boss, Chris Williams, has a framework for how to create an action log within a meeting:

- Delegate one person who is not a main presenter in the meeting to be the note-taker. This person is responsible for filling out the action plan in the meeting.

- If possible, project the action plan onto a second screen as the presenter uses the primary screen. This allows everyone to see real-time updates to the action plan and chime in with questions or corrections.

- During the last five to ten minutes of the meeting, have the note-taker or main presenter read the action plan to the group. Everyone will leave the meeting on the same page about what actions will be taken and by whom.

- Email the action plan to meeting attendees and all other applicable parties following the meeting.

Action plans can be created at any time. Your team could develop an action plan in preparation for a meeting or create an action plan after a meeting to recap and figure out how to move forward. Also, you don't need to wait for a scheduled meeting to update an action plan. Action plans can be updated and shared in real-time through programs like Google Docs and Google Sheets.

Action plans are most effective when they are kept up to date. Updating action plans may entail closing out completed actions and adding new ones. As goals are met, create new goals to keep improving. Never sit back and be satisfied with your results. If you are doing great and crushing it, create a plan to take it to an even higher level.

Use action plans to recap meetings, identify specific actions to be taken, assign responsibility, and keep everyone updated on progress toward goals. When you use action plans, you will be more organized and prepared for follow-up communication.

Once you get the YES, be sure to plan your post-game. It's never in your best interest to get the YES and then go dark. After getting the YES, continually follow up with data-informed feedback. Using data and action plans shows you can be trusted and are serious about following through on the promises and claims you made when making the ask.

Never underestimate the power of the post-game. Follow-up assures your customer that they made the right decision and increases the likelihood you will get a YES in the future.

BE TRUSTWORTHY

Some time ago, the Buyer at a large retailer praised me for always bringing them hard data to back up my recommendations. The Buyer complained that my competitor, the Head of Sales at a different beer supplier, seemed like a slimy salesman and routinely failed to follow through on his promises. Years later, this competitor applied for an open position on my team. Not only had I heard about him from the Buyer, but having worked in the same category, I saw first-hand how careless and unprincipled he was. I chose not to even interview him. I need trustworthy people on my team, and this fellow had already proven we didn't share the same values.

How do you show trustworthiness? First, don't insist that someone trust you. Instead, demonstrate you can be trusted by backing up what you say. Have data to support your claims. In the same regard, don't pressure someone into believing you because you showed them data in the past. You should continually have updated data that supports your claims.

You can also demonstrate trustworthiness by being true to your word. When you say you're going to do something, do it. Call when you say you're going to call. Follow up when you say you're going to follow up. People will feel more comfortable trusting you with bigger things once you have shown you can be trusted to follow through with small, everyday things.

Being trustworthy is paramount when making the ask. If you are not seen as trustworthy, people will always second guess whether the terms you're presenting are fair because no one wants to feel like they were taken advantage of or had the wool pulled over their eyes. Master negotiator Chris Von noted that your audience might even take a "less optimal deal" if they feel they are being treated fairly (and destroy a deal they don't deem fair, even if it results in them losing money).[4] In other words, being trustworthy can lead you to a more advantageous deal and a more satisfied client.[5]

While people might not come out and say someone is trustworthy, they almost certainly take note when someone proves untrustworthy. Make sure you do not lose the trust of your decision-maker. Be reliable. Be consistent and use data to support your claims. Be known for being trustworthy.

CREATE CONNECTION

I remember meeting with the Buyers of a local grocery store chain in Arkansas to sell Teavana Ready-to-Drink Iced Tea into their stores. After mentioning that I had come in from New York City, I spent the first ten minutes answering their questions about NYC and how it was to live there. They were more interested in NYC than the product I was selling. So, even though we had limited time, we spent time engaging with them to strengthen our relationship.

A positive relationship is key when striving to get the YES. When there is a familiarity between business associates, you are more likely to give each other the benefit of the doubt. At times, I've found that even with the most spectacular product, it was hard to get a YES from the Buyer if we didn't have a personal connection. So, whether it's chatting with a business associate about where they went to college or taking a few minutes before a presentation to talk with members of your audience, find opportunities to connect.[6] Never rely on only a personal connection to get the YES, but strive to build a personal connection to get an edge.

One way to grow personal connection is through small talk. Small talk can sometimes feel intimidating and awkward. However, the reward is worth the initial discomfort. When you consistently skip small talk, you consistently miss out on opportunities to create connection. (Although small talk can be helpful most of the time, some people just want to get down to business. It is important to sense when your client wants to skip small talk and respect that.)

If you're unsure about how to begin chatting, ask a question. Try inquiring about things you truly want to know or find interesting, rather than asking every person the same question, for example about their weekend plans or the weather. And if you ask someone a question, show interest in their answer. This will result in more authentic, memorable, and meaningful conversations.

Another way to initiate small talk is by sharing something about yourself. For example, a humorous, self-deprecating story can be helpful in putting others at ease and reducing tension. I remember my client beginning a meeting at Gopuff's Philadelphia office with "On the way here, I didn't get off at the right exit and ended up on the bridge to New Jersey." We spent the first few minutes of the meeting talking about the mishap and laughing about how it has happened to me, too (on a few occasions).

Regardless of the specifics of a conversation, it is important to *listen* when the other person talks. Help them continue *their* conversation, whether it is through sharing personal information, asking questions, or, most importantly, validating that you understand what they're saying. Vanessa Van Edwards' book *Captivate* is a great resource for anyone wanting to improve their skills in building connections.[7]

I suggest keeping personal information that you learn about a client (e.g., names of spouse and children, favorite sports teams, location of a vacation home) in your contacts. You never know when you'll be interacting with them again, so it's good to have the info easily available. (Once you make a personal connection, you may become their go-to person within your company and end up speaking with them more than expected!) Refer to this information before speaking again.

A good personal relationship can equal a good working relationship. The more you know someone, their perspective, and what they are looking for, the better you can sell to them. Don't rely on a personal connection, but use connections to your advantage to get the YES.

RECAP

Getting the YES is not a one-time thing. You will need to get the YES time and time again, so it's important to get good at it. Here's how:

- Always be prepared to make an ask. Know what you want, and be clear in your requests.

- Know who the decision-maker is, and tailor your presentation to that person or team.

- Come prepared with data to state your case and support your recommendations.

- Use a win-win approach when you negotiate.

- Follow through after getting the YES. Create an action plan that shows how and when you will meet goals.

- Connect personally with your audience to facilitate trust and collaboration.

You won't get a YES every time, but don't let that get you down. When someone thinks about you (and whether or not you're ready for a promotion) they will remember how you communicated, reacted, and carried yourself, not the specifics of a negotiation. When you present yourself as competent and trustworthy, you will come out ahead and grow in your career.

CHAPTER 9

PRESENT LIKE A PRO

I HAVE SAT THROUGH HUNDREDS and hundreds of presentations. Many were horrible. Most were boring. When you pull off a great presentation, your colleagues will remember it, appreciate it, and think highly of you.

Whether in person or on video, in front of five or 500 people, presentations are when people get to know you and see what you're all about. Most people won't ever see what you do when you're working by yourself at your desk. In contrast, when you do a presentation, your work is seen by your coworkers, your managers, and managers from other departments (the same managers who could be interviewing you for your next position).

Whether you're answering a question, introducing a best practice, or making an ask, you will often be doing so with a presentation. Don't just give a humdrum presentation. Instead, give a presentation that will leave a lasting impression, get you the YES, and positively impact your career.

Presentation skills are a very powerful skill set to have. Accordingly, I have dedicated an entire chapter to helping you present like a pro. The information in this chapter will help you create great decks, engage your audience, pivot when appropriate, set up your screen or stage, and stay on schedule.

The best opportunity to make a positive, memorable impression is during a presentation. This is your time to shine. So, put your best foot forward, bring your A-game, and present like a pro.

DESIGN YOUR DECK

Most of my presentations have included a Google Slides or PowerPoint deck. In addition to helping communicate your message, a well-crafted deck shows that you put forethought into your presentation. It also provides a handy recap you can forward to your boss, team, or audience.

As you design your deck, keep these tips in mind:

- As a rule of thumb, a thirty-minute presentation should have no more than fifteen slides. A ten-minute presentation should have five to six slides. Fewer slides are usually better than more.

- You don't want a slide with too many words on it. Don't paste blocky paragraphs onto your slides.

- Consider short, bullet-pointed sentences. They can serve as reminders for what to discuss next but should not be read verbatim.[1]

- Prepare additional information to share that's not on the slide. I personally love adding "fun facts."

- Make sure your font is big enough for everyone in your audience to read. Small font is one of the most common errors I notice during in-person presentations. And if the font is big and grainy (from a zoomed-in screenshot), that's also no good. Err on the side of visual clarity.

- Don't display a spreadsheet with copious rows and numbers. The font will end up being too small. If you do include a spreadsheet, highlight, bold, or use bright colors on the words and numbers you want emphasized.

- Anticipate what questions will be asked and prepare answers to those questions. You can incorporate that information into your presentation. This could be done by saying, "A question you may have is . . . and here is the answer . . ." (This approach comes off as personable and connects you to the audience because it shows that you are taking their point of view.) Or you could create additional slides for backup and use only if a particular question is asked.

- Once you have designed your deck, you can focus on the mechanics of how you will present.

SOUND SPONTANEOUS

Don't simply read your presentation. I can immediately tell from the tone and cadence of a person's voice if they're reading a speech, even if I can't see them. While you may have an amazing speech (because every word has been meticulously thought through), a speech that sounds like it's being read verbatim will end up being stale.[2] In contrast, when it sounds like you are making it up as you go along, your audience will be on the edge of their seats because, in essence, *anything can happen!*[3]

Sounding spontaneous doesn't mean not practicing. On the contrary, it usually requires a lot of rehearsal. Sims Wyeth, the President of an executive development firm focused on public speaking, notes that "actors train for years to be able to make written scripts sound 'real' or conversational."[4] If you're not a professional actor or don't have weeks to perfect a memorized speech, there still are a number of things you can do to keep your audience on their toes.

First, gain a strong understanding of your material. Wyeth calls this "Internalizing the Message."[5] Have a sound idea of what information you want to share and the order in which you plan to present it. Then, during your presentation, talk from your head instead of from a script. This will enable your words and tone of voice to sound more spontaneous. [6]

Second, make impromptu, real-time comments about yourself, your audience, or the environment. Stanford Lecturer Dan Klein encourages speakers to "use something from the room in your talk" so your presentation is specific "to that space and . . . time."[7] An excellent time to do this is right before you present. After introducing yourself (if the audience doesn't know you) and what you are going to talk about, crack a joke about something in the environment, comment on the previous speaker, or ask the audience a question.

If you are presenting to your team (likely the bulk of your presentations) and know everyone in the room by name, find a way to incorporate them into your presentation. For example, "This idea is similar to the one Molly presented during last week's meeting." This shows that you are in the moment, engaging with your audience in real time. It also keeps your audience attentive because everyone perks up when they hear their name.

Third, have key points written down in your notes. In the past, when I "memorized" my speech and didn't use notes, I ended up forgetting at least one important point. Therefore, I recommend having notes that include 5–10 bullet points. When I have these reminders on hand, I am more likely to remember to include them (and less worried about leaving them out).

Fourth, make eye contact. It makes things feel more personable. As a presenter, when I prioritize making eye contact, I am less "in my head" and do a better job connecting with my audience This could be because eye contact triggers your body to react as if you are engaging in a conversation and has a relaxing effect on your whole demeanor. This leads to you and your audience being more engaged.[8]

Eye contact not only helps your audience feel like you're speaking directly to them, but it also provides you with valuable feedback. Is everyone following along? Do they look confused? Does anyone have questions? Making eye contact enables you to receive non-verbal information from your audience and adapt your presentation accordingly.[9]

When presenting virtually, eye contact is difficult, if not impossible (especially when you can't see your audience or it's a big group). Moreover, if your audience is on mute, you won't hear any "mmm hmms" to indicate whether they are following along and in agreement. For those reasons, when I present virtually, I generally pause after every slide to ask for feedback. I stop and ask if anyone has questions or comments. I may say, "Does anyone have any questions or comments?" five times during a fifteen-minute speech.

Don't think of your presentation as a one-way street. You want to engage with your audience.[10] This will make your presentation sound more spontaneous and, in turn, help your audience receive your message.

Don't read from a script, but also don't "wing" a presentation. Prepare for presentations like you prepare for other important things. When you speak fluently about your topic and engage with your audience, you can communicate your message effectively.

BE PREPARED TO PIVOT

I once had a meeting with the Buyer of a local family-run grocery store chain in the Midwest, to whom I was trying to sell Teavana Ready-to-Drink Iced Tea. I attended the meeting with the local wholesaler, who had a personal relationship with the grocery store Buyer. We went into the Buyer's office and made small talk for the first five minutes.

As I pulled out the hard copy of my PowerPoint presentation, I noticed the Buyer's head shake ever-so-slightly and sensed that this person did not want to review a twenty-page deck but preferred to have a casual conversation. You could say he was old school (in a good way). Immediately, without hesitation, I put my PowerPoint presentation handout back into my bag and recited my slides from memory.

My intuition and quick response may have paid off. The Buyer accepted Teavana right there in the meeting. The moral of the story: You should really know your material and be prepared to adjust your presentation on the fly to match different audiences' needs and preferences.

Try to read your audience, and be prepared to pivot your style and language to match them. If your audience didn't understand the complex words you used or the analyses you presented, the content of whatever you just said was lost. I have been in many situations where my boss or colleague was presenting to a retailer, and I could tell the retailer was lost because the idea was presented with too much complexity. The retailers often looked to me to simplify, which I was typically able to do.

You may also need to pivot when a meeting is running late and you won't have your full time to present. There have been many times when I had a thirty-minute meeting scheduled with a senior leader from our company, but at the beginning of the call, they say, "I only have fifteen minutes to talk." In these situations, I've had to quickly adjust.

If I know before beginning that I won't have time to get through the presentation, I identify the most important issues (and slides) and only go over those. I usually prefer to take out less important items rather than rush through more important concepts and risk them being unclear. Since it is common for meetings to get cut short, I typically go into meetings with a list of things I would like to address, in order of priority. If I don't get through the list, I can send a follow-up email when appropriate with the other issues I didn't get to.

Relatedly, if you are presenting at a conference or within a longer meeting, double-check on the time allotted for your presentation. Sometimes there are last-minute agenda changes. I recommend reaching out to the organizer forty-eight hours in advance to ensure the time you were initially told is still correct.

I occasionally find myself needing to pivot when there is a lot of unanticipated discussion. Sometimes, one question turns into another question (and another). At some point, you need to decide whether to transition back to your presentation or continue the dialogue and risk not showing your other slides.

While how you handle a presentation is always situation-specific, in most cases, I recommend abandoning your other slides and going deeper into a discussion if your audience is passionate about the issue. If you have the flexibility, build upon the energy and inquisitiveness of your audience.

Finally, it is important to pivot if your audience requires a particular presentation style. For example, not all companies use slide decks. Some companies are transitioning to a presentation style called "White Paper" in lieu of decks. This style involves communicating through a 6-page written narrative. Gopuff uses this model for internal presentations. It may be useful to familiarize yourself with this presentation style in case you need to create or participate in this style of presentation.[11]

A last-minute pivot can be challenging and frustrating (especially if you end up having to ditch amazing slides). Still, you need to be flexible and able to change your presentation at a moment's notice. A swift pivot can possibly save your presentation and help your career.

SET UP FOR SUCCESS

When you're in the middle of presenting, you don't want to be concerned with and distracted by whether your audience can see your screen or hear your voice. So, before it's "go time," put time and energy into setting up your stage for an in-person presentation or your computer screen for a virtual presentation. Little things you do ahead of time can help presentations go smoothly and prevent snafus that can throw you off your game.

Here are some tips to help you set up your presentation and get off to a great start.

SET UP YOUR SCREEN – VIRTUAL PRESENTATION TIPS

- If you are leading a virtual meeting, log on one minute early so you have time to share your screen and get your deck ready. I have been in numerous important thirty-minute meetings where the lead presenter didn't attempt to share their screen until about five minutes after start time. A couple more minutes ended up being wasted due to difficulty screen sharing. Now it's seven minutes into the meeting, and the presenter ends up rushing through a thirty-minute presentation so they can finish in twenty-three minutes.

- If you have two monitors, put your deck on one monitor and your bulleted pointed notes, or an outline of your presentation, on the other monitor.

- When presenting a deck, be sure to be in Presentation mode, so your slides are easier to see.

- Use headphones to help with sound quality, if it's noisy where you are or your computer's microphone is sometimes not great.

SET UP THE STAGE – IN-PERSON PRESENTATION TIPS

- Speak loud enough for everyone to hear. If a microphone is provided, please use it. Many people don't want to use a microphone but then end up using it after two minutes when the back of the room can't hear. You may think you have a loud voice, but a microphone will ensure the entire audience can hear you.

- If you're projecting your deck onto a big screen:
  - Know the process for connecting your computer and getting your presentation onto the screen. If your meeting room is booked right up until the time of your presentation, you won't have much time for setup. I recommend going to the conference room early in the day or during off-hours, if possible, to practice setting up.

  - In addition to having your deck on the big screen, have your presentation up on a computer in front of you. This way, you can glance at your slides, if necessary, instead of looking behind you at the screen.

  - When presenting, stand on the right side of the stage or "stage right." (In theater lingo, "stage right" means the actor's right but the audience's left.) I learned this in 2007 on the first day of my first MBA class at the University of Arkansas and have since followed it during every one of my presentations. Why stand to the audience's left? Because we read from left to right. As the audience looks to the screen to read, they first see the presenter on the left and then read from left to right. If the presenter is on the right, it's more difficult for the audience to focus on the presenter and then back to the screen to read. Even if the podium is on the left side of the stage and every other presenter has stood at that podium for their presentation, I present from the right side of the stage (and move the podium if I can).

STAY ON SCHEDULE

Whether you're in person or virtual, presenting to three people or to 300, when you lead a meeting, start and stop on time.

If I am presenting or leading a meeting, I always strive to start on time. If someone's late, too bad; they miss the opening. I believe in starting on time rather than waiting for stragglers because it shows respect to the punctual participants.

Likewise, if you are leading a meeting, end on time. I do everything in my power to end meetings on time or even a few minutes early. This allows attendees to get to their next meeting on time.

The logistics surrounding working remotely can amplify the need to stay on schedule. When working remotely, it is not uncommon for almost 90% of my day to be scheduled with back-to-back virtual meetings. If one meeting veers off schedule, it can negatively impact my whole day.

If you think your presentation will likely run over the allotted time, inform your audience. When I'm leading a meeting and it's running over, I alert everyone at least fifteen minutes before the scheduled end time. I hate being in meetings that run thirty minutes to an hour over, and the leader doesn't recognize that we are running late. Be honest with your attendees if the meeting is expected to run late, so they will know how the change will impact their day. When appropriate, let your audience know it's okay if they need to leave or drop off early.

Preparation and practice are key for staying on schedule. When preparing your presentation, anticipate questions that may be asked, and allot time in your presentation to address those and other questions. Also, practice your presentation aloud so you know how long it will actually take to get through your slides. There is nothing worse than going over by twenty minutes because you didn't properly rehearse your timing.

All eyes are on you when you present. So, use this opportunity to show you have what it takes to not just present a deck but to also lead a meeting. When you stay on schedule, it demonstrates preparation, organization, and professionalism. These are qualities that will help you stand out and get you promoted.

It takes practice and hard work to become a skilled presenter. I've been doing it my whole career and am still disappointed with many of my presentations. However, getting positive feedback about a presentation can be very motivating and encourages me to continually try to make each presentation great. No, not just great, but amazing.

I received this email from someone I didn't know, who had watched one of my presentations at the Beverage Digest Future's Smart Conference in December 2017.

HEY RANDY,

I really enjoyed your presentation Friday afternoon in NYC. Very refreshing. Very real. Thanks for your candor and your respect for your audience. I got the feeling that you've been victimized by lame presenters in your career and that you have decided to be different.

This note made my day. It meant my presentation was exactly what I had gone for. I wanted my presentation to stand out from boring ones and give my audience something they would remember. Practice your presentations, and maybe you will get a note like this someday, too.

RECAP

Most of you will give presentations in your job. It pays to make them the best they can be. Here's how to present like a pro:

- Keep your deck to a minimum number of slides and make each one count.

- Limit the words on each slide, and share additional information not on the slides.

- Know your material. When you know your subject matter well, you can speak spontaneously about a subject and not have to rely on reading from a script.

- Engage your audience by making and maintaining eye contact and answering questions.

- Stand to the audience's left so their eyes can travel more easily from left to right across the screen.

- Be open to adapting your presentation to help communicate your message.

- Start and end on time; respect the schedules of those in attendance.

- Master the art of presenting well. As your presentation skills grow, so will your career.

CHAPTER 10

INVEST IN YOUR FUTURE

DECISIONS WE MAKE and actions we take early in our careers set in motion future opportunities and advantages. Accordingly, it is critical to put ourselves in environments that are promising, supportive, and full of potential. Seek out mentors, build friendships, risk relocation, and take advantage of job opportunities. These are key ways to invest in your career.

MEET WITH A MENTOR

I've had several junior coworkers ask me to be their mentor, and I considered every request an honor. I tried to have monthly meetings with my mentees, whether it was during lunch, happy hour, or regular work hours. We discussed how their job was going, potential opportunities, and occasionally even their personal lives. I feel proud to have supported their career journeys.

Asking someone to be a mentor can be intimidating, especially when done outside of a formal mentorship program. Despite the initial discomfort, I recommend going for it. Start by identifying someone you admire who is at least one level higher than you. Send them a message to schedule a time to meet, preferably in person. The message doesn't have to be complex. It could be short:

"I am looking for a mentor in the company, and I've always valued your feedback. Can we schedule a time to meet and talk more?"

Once they agree to be your mentor, move forward with scheduling monthly thirty-minute meetings. Make it as easy as possible for the mentor. Initiate the calendar invites or meetings yourself rather than expecting the mentor to do this.

If you're not getting the attention you would like from your mentor, or you feel like you're just not meshing, find someone else. It's not an "until death do us part" relationship. Many people out there enjoy and find fulfillment from being mentors.

Not all mentor–mentee relationships will develop so formally. Some will develop naturally over time from relationships with people in your company, or sometimes outside of your company but in the same field. You may find yourself going to the same person(s) for career advice or formal recommendations. A relationship doesn't have to be officially labeled as mentor–mentee, and it's okay to have multiple informal mentors. What is important is that you are getting the guidance you need when you need it.

A current mentor of mine is someone who used to be my boss. As a boss, he was never shy about giving me feedback and calling me out on things I did wrong. He also consistently asked me about myself, my interests, and my family. Even after I no longer reported to him, I went back to him for advice and began to view him more as a mentor.

I didn't consider him to be my mentor when he was boss. Nor would I recommend for your boss to be your mentor. It is helpful to have someone who you can speak candidly to about people and situations on your team. If there's something you don't want to tell your boss about, your mentor can be a sounding board and can offer an objective but well-informed opinion.

When I left A-B, I confided in my mentor about the different jobs I was considering. We discussed the pros and cons of each opportunity. A few years later, he was the one to call me for input and career guidance. A mentor can eventually evolve into a colleague, peer, and friend. The characteristics of each mentor–mentee relationship will, of course, vary depending on your personalities, your company, your career needs, and the amount of time you dedicate to the relationship.

A mentor often can provide you with valuable insight into your company. My own mentor, for example, was better than my boss when it came to helping me navigate the various departments and know whom I should go to for different issues within our large organization. A mentor can also help you figure out how to move up in the company and advocate for you as you prepare for promotion. A mentor is usually well-connected and can help boost your relationships with others in the organization. For each of my mentees, I spoke with hiring managers and provided positive recommendations. I even hired and promoted two of them myself.

The mentor–mentee relationship is not just advantageous for the mentee. There are also benefits to being a mentor. The relationship can help a mentor hone their management skills (the things mentors and mentees discuss are often the same types of things a manager talks about with their direct reports). Furthermore, providing support has psychological benefits—even more than one gets from receiving support![1]

You're not going to get to the top all by yourself. You are going to need to utilize available resources—and that includes other people. Don't just rely on informal relationships with people in your everyday social circle at work. You need to go above and beyond and find yourself a mentor. A mentor typically has had a successful career and can provide guidance on how they got promoted. In fact, they may reiterate and expand upon lessons you read about in this book.

FACILITATE FRIENDSHIPS

One of the greatest—and sometimes most beneficial—ways to invest in your future is through facilitating friendships at work. Your coworkers are people who you may eat with, travel with, come to rely on, and need to trust. As you work with the same people day after day, year after year, it is natural for friendships to develop. Some of my best friends are people I've met through work. Whether you call them friends, colleagues, or coworkers, these are the people who make your days more enjoyable and whom you can call on in a heartbeat. A strong network of friends at your company and within your industry can serve you well throughout your career.

A good way to make work friends is by strengthening your relationship with coworkers whom you regularly go to for help—the coworkers whom you go to for assistance and resources (i.e., data requests, ideas, software assistance). When you strengthen these ties, whether it's through going to lunch or just talking about nonwork things, you build trust. And this makes working together and communicating easier and more enjoyable.[2]

When I was VP of Walmart Sales at A-B, I became friends with Stewart, who worked in our Revenue Management Department as a Pricing and Promotions Analyst. He was my dedicated resource for pricing and analytics and became my go-to for most of my data-related questions and projects. Stewart and I both lived in St. Louis, drove down to Bentonville together on multiple occasions, and ate meals together. The time that we spent together strengthened our relationship. We got to know and trust each other.

I felt comfortable assigning Stewart big projects because I knew he had the ability and dedication to complete the tasks. Correspondingly, he was excited to receive my requests and worked hard to complete them, in part because he wanted to please and impress me. I was able to assist Stewart in receiving a deserving promotion on more than one occasion.

After I left A-B, Stewart reached out to me. He was looking for career advice related to starting his own company. After getting his company off the ground, Stewart contacted me for managerial and personnel-related guidance. Reaching out after we no longer worked together was an ultimate move on his part to strengthen our friendship. I was happy and honored that he did and that I was able to help. I don't know at what point Stewart and I became friends in addition to coworkers. However, that "extra ingredient of friendship" helped us both enjoy work, improve our performance, and strengthen our careers.

Work friendships are not guaranteed to be as harmonious and drama free as my friendship with Stewart. It is always necessary to be aware of how boundaries, power differentials, and conflicts of interest can impact even the most platonic work relationships. It is also vital to be aware of your company's policies related to socializing outside of work.*

While it is critical to continually be aware of and monitor risks related to having work friends, if you become overly fixated on

---

*For more information on how to appropriately socialize with coworkers, see Hailey Shafir, "How to Socialize with Coworkers at Work," SocialSelf, March 7, 2022, https://socialself.com/blog/socialize-work/

potential pitfalls of friendships or are just too closed off at work, you may be missing out on many positive benefits that go along with workplace friendships.[3] It is probably in your best interest to not be "a passing ship in the night" at work. Instead, get to know your coworkers and invest in those relationships.

Make an effort to put yourself in places that are conducive to interacting and building relationships with your coworkers. Lunchtime is a great time to connect with coworkers. If you brought your lunch to the office, don't sit at your desk to eat. Go sit in the kitchen or a communal space. If you're going out for lunch, invite some coworkers to join. Try to eat with more than the same few people within your team by including people you don't see as often from other departments. Similarly, during happy hours, company-wide events, and conferences, don't just talk to your best work friends. Move outside your comfort zone. Start conversations with others instead of relying on people to approach you.

Helping coworkers is another great way to reinforce positive relationships. When people help one another, friendships can naturally evolve and strengthen. Reinforce relationships by helping your coworkers and coming to their rescue.

While it's natural for friendships to develop with those you work with most closely, having friends in other departments can also be particularly helpful. The more connections you have in your overall organization, the easier it is to access information, obtain resources, and get cross-functional support when you need it, such as when completing a best practice.

Reinforcing relationships with colleagues at different companies within your industry or profession is also advantageous. If you are in a specialized industry like mine (the beverage industry and, even more broadly, consumer packaged goods) you end up interacting with the same folks throughout your career. Friends within your industry but who work at different companies can come in particularly handy if you are looking to hire new talent or exploring taking a new position yourself.

To build and strengthen work relationships, you don't need to even spend time together outside of work. I spent over nine years working with Walmart and became friendly with many of their employees. While I didn't meet up with their Buyers outside of work (Walmart has strict rules surrounding socializing with suppliers), I got to know them and developed their trust through consistently and effectively helping them find solutions and reach their goals.

I stay in touch with many people from work with whom I built relationships. These are people I consider friends and whom I can call on at any time for help or advice. When you build, nurture, and maintain work relationships, you gain an extensive support network within your industry, people with a trove of resources at their disposal who can help you grow in your career both now and in the future.

BE WILLING TO RELOCATE

Relocating is hard. Life's complexities (e.g., marriage, children, mortgage, aging parents, and so on) can make relocating challenging and often undesirable. However, in many large companies (especially those with offices all over the country and world), it has historically been very difficult to move up the ladder while staying in the same office or city.

My wife and I decided early in our marriage that we would relocate to any city, even internationally, if it made sense for my career. In total, I have relocated five times: Chicago to St. Louis; St. Louis to Northwest Arkansas; Northwest Arkansas back to St. Louis; St. Louis to New York City; and New York City to Philadelphia.

With more and more roles becoming remote, relocation has become less of an issue for some. However, the need for relocation has not gone away. Employees will continually be given the opportunity to relocate and face the decision about whether or not to move.

I know people who have turned down multiple promotions because they didn't want or weren't able to move to a particular city. You can probably turn down a promotion that requires a relocation once and not experience any negative effects. However, if you turn down multiple promotions within the same company because you don't want to relocate, you will be overlooked for future promotions and miss out on opportunities for advancement. (You may be better off leaving that particular company if you don't want to remain stagnant in your role.)

I have known people who have moved ten and even fifteen times in their careers. It can be stressful, but if you can handle the moves, I recommend taking advantage of the opportunities afforded with relocation. Here are some benefits, beyond a promotion, that can come from relocation:

• Relocation can help you become a stronger candidate for future roles. Moving locations will likely broaden your skills and market knowledge. For example, if you are in a consumer packaged goods (CPG) sales role, I believe it's better to work on two different accounts for five years each than work with one account for ten years. After working

on the same account for too many years, you learn fewer
new things. Also, as you move around, you tend to meet
more coworkers and make more connections, which can be
an asset when looking for your next role.

• You can make money relocating. If you own a home, you
  can often make money when you sell. If you move to
  a more expensive market, you may get a cost-of-living
  adjustment incorporated into your new salary. Your
  company's relocation policy may contain other financial
  incentives such as a large stipend for moving expenses,
  reimbursement for closing costs on a home, or a monetary
  bonus if your house sells quickly.

• Living in different places can be enriching. You learn about
  other parts of the country (or world), make new friends,
  and experience different cultures. Plus, you get to try all
  different types of foods, which is my favorite. I have found
  the best hotdogs in Chicago, the best BBQ in St. Louis,
  the best steak and Thai food in Arkansas, the best bagels
  and pizza in New York, and the best Chinese food—and
  of course, cheesesteaks—in Philadelphia. (Yes, I said Thai
  food in Arkansas. You'd be surprised.)

In many large national companies, it is not uncommon to, at
some point, get relocated to a small city (e.g., Bentonville, Arkansas; Topeka, Kansas; Sioux City, Iowa; Fargo, North Dakota; etc.).
I was living in St. Louis, working for IRI, when I interviewed
with A-B for a Category Space Manager position based out of
Dallas. After the interview, my future boss told me, "You can try
and go for the Dallas position, and you may or may not get it. Or

we have the same job open in Bentonville, Arkansas. If you want to move to Arkansas, the job is yours." I took the job, which ended up being a critical career move.

Being open to living in a small city can help you move up quickly in a company, especially if you're willing to accept a position that others may pass up.

My former direct report (who is now also my friend) Chris grew up in Fort Lee, New Jersey, outside of New York City. He worked in NYC for PepsiCo after college. Early in his career with Pepsi, he had a promotional opportunity within the company to manage an account for a major Midwest grocery store chain. He took a leap of faith and relocated to Des Moines, Iowa. It was a city he had never been to and where he didn't know anyone.

This wound up becoming a great career move for him. I hired him to work at A-B partly because of his experience working in different parts of the country and his openness to relocate. He ended up moving back to NYC when he took the job with A-B. However, when the pandemic hit and he could work remotely, he chose to move (at least temporarily) back to Des Moines once his NYC lease was up.

I have seen many employees, including myself, enjoy their experiences relocating, whether it was to a small city, to a city they had never been to, or to a city where they didn't know anyone. Growing up in South Florida, I never thought I would live in Arkansas. I didn't know one person who had lived there and wasn't even certain I could find it on a map before I moved there.

Still, I lived there for six years, received my MBA from the University of Arkansas (Woo Pig Sooie!), and met great friends, many of whom worked at different CPG companies, and with whom I continue to cross paths. I have also seen numerous coworkers relocate to A-B's Bentonville office and then leave A-B so they could continue living in Arkansas rather than transfer out of the area.

Deciding whether or not to relocate is a very personal decision influenced by individual and situation-specific circumstances. Still, I recommend being open to moving. Relocating can provide unique opportunities for career advancement and other unexpected benefits. If you don't see yourself continually relocating, try relocating early in your career. It will allow you to take advantage of the benefits and see whether or not it's for you. While relocation can be stressful, daunting, and uncharted, the return on your career investment may be worth it.

BE OPEN TO CLIMBING A NEW LADDER

At many points in your career, you will need to decide whether to change jobs. In essence, you will have to choose whether to "climb a new ladder." A new role may be in a different department or a different company. Whatever the specifics, it is important to be open to these opportunities.

It's common to be offered a new role in the same department. Taking the new position is usually a no-brainer and something I recommend, as it's typically a promotion and a natural progression from your previous role.

I also recommend taking advantage of opportunities to move around within a company. Working in different departments gives you a better understanding of how a company operates, which is a very desirable asset. Also, experience in multiple departments introduces you to more people within a company. This can offer immediate benefits, such as when working cross-functionally, and long-term benefits by contributing to a broader professional network.

Staying within your company and moving departments can often provide you with a more diverse experience than you would get by moving corporations. For example, if you work as a Key Account Manager at A-B on their Walmart team and you leave to be a Key Account Manager at Molson Coors on their Walmart team, you're not gaining much experience-wise. In contrast, if you stayed at A-B and moved to their Kroger team, you would be gaining broader experience because you would be working with a different retailer. As a hiring manager in the alcohol category, I generally prefer candidates with broad, diverse experiences.

Eventually, you will consider moving companies. I started climbing a new ladder when I joined Gopuff in 2019. At that point, I had worked at A-B for fifteen years in multiple departments. Working at Gopuff allowed me to expand my experience even further by working for a retailer instead of a supplier. Working for a small growing company with its pulse on the future as an online retailer is also captivating and exciting.

The process of deciding when or whether to change jobs is not going to be necessarily easy or clear-cut. When weighing the pros and cons of different companies, you're not always comparing apples to apples, and your optimal personal career trajectory may not be linear. For example, although I had been in multiple VP positions at A-B, I accepted a director-level role at Gopuff. My new salary was also significantly less than what I earned at A-B. Still, I saw the long-term financial and career-building opportunities at Gopuff, and I took a chance.

Deciding whether to change companies or even roles within a company can be very difficult and deeply personal. I recommend considering the following questions when contemplating a change:

- What skills will you be able to gain in a new role that could help you reach your long-term career goals?

- Do either your current or new roles have opportunities for advancement?

- What is the corporation's size? Do you want to be in a place with less bureaucracy?

- What is the company's culture, such as regarding working on the weekend and traveling?

- What are the long-term and short-term financial benefits or costs?

When you interview for a new role (whether it is with your current company or a different one), capitalize on the lessons in this book. Be sure to share your knowledge of numbers, skills in data analytics, and best practices. Once you become a strong employee, you will be prepared to handle whatever interview questions are thrown your way.

There are many people who, especially early in their career, move frequently from company to company. This is a good way to increase salary and learn a breadth of skills. I sometimes ask myself if I should have left A-B and moved to a different company earlier in my career. While there is no way to know for sure, had I not first climbed the ladder at A-B, I probably wouldn't have had the skill set or financial flexibility to take the position at Gopuff.

Just because you move companies doesn't mean you are

growing. I have seen employees move from one company to another company after being unsuccessful in their previous positions. At the new company, they often run into the same challenges, the same people problems, and the same time management difficulties. If you think this might be you, start by implementing the strategies in this book. I also recommend going through past evaluations from your current and former employers. What did they point out as your weaknesses? What did they identify as areas for improvement? If you're interested in one-on-one assistance in these areas, there are a growing number of career coaches and career consultants who specialize in helping employees improve and thrive at work.

If you have implemented the strategies in this book and you're still not seeing career growth or your current company does not feel right, definitely be open to climbing a new ladder. It could be your situation, rather than yourself, that needs improving.

RECAP

- Find a mentor, even if your company doesn't offer an official mentorship program. Identify someone at least one level higher who you admire, and message them with your request. Follow through with regular meetings with your mentor.

- Get to know your coworkers. Building relationships with colleagues in your company and throughout your industry can result in a trove of resources that can be used throughout your career.

- Be open to relocating, even if it means moving to a place you can't yet find on a map. If you turn down too many relocation offers, your company may pass you over when it comes to promotions.

- Consider climbing a new career ladder. Sometimes this means taking a job on a lower rung in another company.

It is important to invest in your future. When you stretch yourself early in your career through finding a mentor, creating friendships, and potentially relocating, you are laying the groundwork for future career growth. While certain factors related to promotion are out of your control, when you have invested in your future by strengthening yourself, your network, and your support system, you will grow and flourish when your time is right.

CONCLUSION

THERE ARE MANY FACTORS outside our control that must fall into place for a promotion to happen. In essence, you must be in the right place, at the right time, with the right experience when there is an opening (e.g., someone in a more senior role has left the company or got promoted). In many cases, it's less about applying for the right position than it is about being the right person when a position becomes available. (Upper management will often identify who they think should fill a role before an opening or any changes are even announced.) So, shine in your current role and be the person leadership thinks of when there is an open position.

Use the strategies in this book to get others to recognize that you are prepared for the next step in your career. These strategies helped me move up the ranks and got me to where I am today in my career. These are the strategies that helped me get promoted. And these are the strategies that will help you get promoted.

Let's review what we learned in this book:

It is important to approach your everyday tasks with urgency, enthusiasm, and excellence:

- Use meetings to their fullest.
- Represent yourself well in written communication.

- Take extra time to learn analytical software and statistics specific to your role. Be able to confidently explain what you know.

- Schedule things with purpose.

- Focus on team goals and building your team up, rather than individual recognition.

Go above and beyond executing your daily job responsibilities. Find ways to improve your company:

- Spearhead a project suggested by your boss or work together with a coworker to improve a process.

- Use data instead of your imagination to find solutions to problems.

- Know your audience. Find out about their goals ahead of time, and tailor your presentation to their needs.

- After getting the YES, follow up with data-supported results.

- Take time to put together engaging presentations.

- Find mentors and create friendships with people who can support and advise you throughout your career.

My tips and tricks are practical things you can do to stand out from the crowd and show your boss you have what it takes to rise to the next level—that you have what it takes to get promoted!

I wish you well on your journey.

APPENDIX 1

INCREMENTAL OPPORTUNITY IS A SALES METRIC I often use when selling an item into a retailer. Incremental opportunity refers to new revenue that will be gained from a new item. In other words, how much additional money will the new item bring to a retailer's total category. (Depending on your situation, you can interchange "new item" with "new program" or "new process.")

A novice in business may mistakenly believe that any grocery store will, of course, benefit monetarily from carrying and selling your new product. However, this is short-sighted. If you are selling a me-too (copy-cat) item or an item that is similar in any way to other items in the store, the dollars generally just transfer from one item to another within the category, an effect called "cannibalization." The more differentiated your item, the smaller the cannibalization rate and the more incremental opportunity it will provide.

There is no perfect way to calculate cannibalization. Every new item will cannibalize an old one to a degree. You just need to estimate by how much.

After working with this data my entire career, I use the following guidelines:

- A "me-too" or copy-cat item (an item that is very similar to an already existing item) has a cannibalization rate of 80–100%. This is an incremental opportunity rate of 0–20%.

- A differentiated item (a new flavor, etc.) has a cannibalization rate of 50–80%. This is an incremental opportunity rate of 20–50%.

- A new-to-the-world item (the first of a product to enter a category) has a 30–50% cannibalization rate. This is an incremental opportunity rate of 50–70%.

- In my opinion, nothing has a cannibalization rate of less than 30% or an incremental opportunity rate of over 70%.

Syndicated data providers (e.g., IRI, Nielsen) can provide their own, potentially more accurate, estimated cannibalization rate based on their data and algorithms. (Don't ask me how they do it; that's why we pay them the big bucks.) Here is an example (with fabricated numbers) of how incremental opportunity could look with a new item in an established category.

If a retailer's BBQ Sauce Category sells $10 million a year and a new Randy's Yellow Curry BBQ Sauce is projected to sell $1 million. $1 million is the *size of the prize*. If the cannibalization rate is projected to be 70%, then the amount of *new* money it would really be bringing into the category (the incremental opportunity) is $300,000—not $1 million. The other $700,000 would be dollars taken away from other BBQ sauces in the category. The retailer's projected BBQ Sauce Category sales will go from $10 million to $10.3 million.

	BBQ Sauce Category	Randy's Yellow Curry BBQ	Cannibalization Rate	Incremental Dollars	BBQ Sauce Projected Dollars
52 Week Dollars	$10,000,000	$1,000,000	70%	$300,000	$10,300,000

If you state that you expect a 30% incrementality rate, you should provide support for your estimation. Support could be as simple as unique facts about your product or as in depth as feedback from a focus group. Whatever your approach, provide some specifics to back up your incrementality estimate.

Incremental opportunity consideration is important, not only when selling to external retailers but also when pitching projects and ideas internally. For example, if a beer brand plans to create a new product, such as a seasonal IPA, they would want to know the incremental opportunity of the new item, given it would likely cannibalize other items in their portfolio.

Whether you're a supplier or a retailer, when you understand incremental opportunity, you will understand the financial benefit of selling highly differentiated items.

APPENDIX 2

JUST LIKE YOU SHOULD KNOW the specific KPIs that affect how your performance is evaluated (see Know Your Numbers), it can be helpful for you to know your decision-makers' KPIs. Some Buyers, for example, are bonused on *gross profit* while others are bonused on *gross profit margins* If you happen to know your Buyer's KPI, you may benefit from tailoring your presentation or pricing to meet their goals.

Some Buyers are bonused on their retailer's *gross profit*, or the amount of money the retailer makes on an item. If the company that makes the energy drink Randy's Rejuvenation sells a bottle to Grocery Mart for $2.40 and Grocery Mart sells it to the consumer for $4.00, Grocery Mart makes $1.60 per bottle sold. Grocery Mart's gross profit is $1.60 per bottle.

Other Buyers are bonused on *gross profit margin percentage*, which is the percentage of the money from net sales that goes to the retailer. For example, if Randy's Rejuvenation is sold to Grocery Mart for $2.40 and Grocery Mart sells it for $4.00, then Grocery Mart makes 40% gross margin ($1.60 is 40% of $4.00). If Grocery Mart's average gross margin percentage for their entire Energy Drink Category is 50%, the Buyer may be more motivated to accept an item to be sold on their shelves if they could make

51% gross profit margin on that item. The 40% gross profit margin that Grocery Mart would make on the $2.40 energy drink being sold for $4.00 might not cut it, as the total category gross margin percent may decline if they brought this item onto their shelves. For the category to maintain a profit margin of 50%, the item would need to be sold for $4.80.

Even though a Buyer may be focused on increasing gross profit margin percentage, a retailer can actually make more money selling a more expensive item with which they receive a smaller gross profit margin percentage than a less expensive item that has a higher gross profit margin percentage. For example, if Value Brand Energy Drink is sold into Grocery Mart for $0.90 and retails for $2.00, it has a 55% gross margin. However, it only brings in $1.10 of gross profit per unit. So, the retailer makes more money when the consumer trades up from Value Brand Energy Drink and buys a premium product like Randy's Rejuvenation ($1.60 brought in vs. $1.10). I have been successful in showing this comparison to get the YES when selling a premium item.

If I'm in a meeting and the Buyer is focusing solely on gross margin percentage, I become leery and wonder if they are just trying to reach their KPI. If that's truly the case, I need to convince them that my product is beneficial to their business, even if that might negatively affect one of their KPIs. Or I can figure out a way to sell my item to them at a lower cost.

Regardless of the specific situation, when you understand the priorities of the person(s) you're trying to influence, you can strategically adjust your approach and increase your odds of getting a YES!

ACKNOWLEDGMENTS

WRITING A BOOK IS NOT AN EASY FEAT. I would like to thank my wife, Hayley Ornstein, for stepping up to help this dream become a reality. She did an amazing job writing while also caring for our children. I can't wait for them to read it as they enter the workforce starting in 2034 and 2037. Hopefully, these tips will remain relevant for years to come.

I thank my parents, Morton and Libbie, who raised me and my brother, Mark, in a family that instilled me with confidence and encouraged hard work and success.

I would like to acknowledge Information Resources (IRI), Anheuser-Busch InBev, and Gopuff. None of my experiences and insights would be possible without them taking a chance on me and recognizing my efforts and performance within their companies. At each company, I gained skills that complemented and facilitated my career growth and development. IRI is where I learned the fundamentals of analyzing and interpreting data. A-B is where I got to lead big teams, create processes, and flourish in the top beverage company in the world. And Gopuff is where I challenged myself to creatively innovate and quickly adapt in a fast-paced ecommerce environment. It has been a privilege to work at all these companies while teaching and supporting junior employees along the way.

I especially want to thank Gopuff co-founders Rafael Ilashayev and Yakir Gola for giving me the opportunity to help Gopuff become the leader in instant needs—the opportunity of a lifetime. Thanks to them, I have developed a stronger appreciation for the power of relationships and continually challenge myself to think and move fast to stay two steps ahead of the competition.

All of my bosses have helped mold me into the person I am today. They provided direction, education, constructive criticism, training, and support. Thank you to my bosses at IRI—Susan Surratt, Lori Williams, Heather Benka; my bosses at A-B—Denny Werner, Terry Hoffman, Mark Franz, Clayton Kotoucek, Mike Potthoff, CJ Watson, Chris Williams, Ari Kertesz, Alexandre Medicis, Brendan Whitworth; and my bosses at Gopuff—Patrick Quire, George Zeefe, (a different) Chris Williams, and Maria Renz.

I have had amazing mentors throughout the years who I was able to depend on for advice and direction. Bump Williams (now at Bump Williams Consulting) was my first mentor when I worked for IRI early in my career. Next was Joe Patti, who led Category Management for A-B and now works at the Partnering Group. Chris Williams and Mike Potthoff were my bosses at A-B during a pivotal part of my career. They treated me like a younger brother, always giving me advice and pushing me to get better. They were the inspiration for many of the best practices in this book. Chris promoted me to my first-ever Vice President position where I led the A-B Walmart/Sam's Club team—a position he previously held. Most recently, David Adelman, business investor and Campus Apartments CEO, who I met after moving to

Philadelphia, has given me advice on how to continue to elevate my brand and my career.

I am thankful to have so many colleagues and friends take an interest in reading my many drafts and provide valuable feedback to improve the content. Thank you to Natalie Marziani, Chris Han, Jack Parker, Shan Pesaru, Bill Donius, Ed Henkler, Amy Griffith, Errol Chapnick, Cassie Finley, and Michael Schwarz.

Ensuring this book was legally compliant was an important hurdle. Thank you to A-B's Vice President and General Counsel Seth Hawkins and Gopuff's Head of Ethics & Compliance and Associate General Counsel Ben Halpert for blessing this book.

Thank you to my publisher, Greenleaf Book Group, for being patient with Hayley and me as we balanced and prioritized work, family, and the pandemic while writing. (Writing during the pandemic enabled the inclusion of more up-to-date content related to working remotely.)

Finally, I want to thank all of my colleagues, peers, direct reports, cross-functional leaders, and senior leaders. There are too many to thank individually, but I learned so much from our constant dialogue.

NOTES

PART 1: EVERYDAY EXCELLENCE

1. Allie Decker, "All About Planograms and Their Role in Visual Merchandising," *Shopify*, February 2, 2022, https://www.shopify.com/retail/planogram-visual-merchandising

2. Abraham Carmeli, Revital Shalom, and Jacob Weisberg, "Considerations in Organizational Career Advancement: What Really Matters," *Personnel Review* 36, no. 2 (2007): 190-205, doi: 10.1108/00483480710726109

CHAPTER 1: MAXIMIZE MEETINGS

1. Daniel H. Pink, "Pitching Like a Pro," *Masterclass* lecture, 2021, https://www.masterclass.com/

2. Abraham Carmeli, Revital Shalom, and Jacob Weisberg, "Considerations in Organizational Career Advancement: What Really Matters," *Personnel Review* 36, no. 2 (2007): 190-205, doi: 10.1108/00483480710726109

CHAPTER 2: MANAGE YOUR MESSAGES

1. Duncan Watts, "Using Digital Data to Shed Light on Team Satisfaction and Other Quotations about Large Organizations," *Organizational Spectroscope*, April 1, 2016, https://medium.com/@duncanjwatts/the-organizational-spectroscope-7f9f239a897c

2. ClientSuccess, "The Sundown Rule & How It Relates to Customer Success," April 26, 2016, https://www.clientsuccess.com/blog/the-sundown-rule-how-it-relates-to-customer-success/

3. Andrew Bloomenthal, "Stock Keeping Unit (SKU)," *Investopedia*, August 5, 2020, https://www.investopedia.com/terms/s/stock-keeping-unit-sku.asp

CHAPTER 3: STUDY FOR SUCCESS

1. Nina Trentmann, "Finance Chiefs Are Still Trying to Replace Excel with New Tools," *Wall Street Journal*, July 21, 2021, https://www.wsj.com/articles/finance-chiefs-are-still-trying-to-replace-excel-with-new-tools-11626859801

2. Chris Westfall, "How to Appear More Intelligent: 5 Ways to Look Smarter Than You Are," *Forbes*, September 16, 2020, https://www.forbes.com/sites/chriswestfall/2020/09/16/how-to-appear-more-intelligent-5-ways-to-look-smarter-than-you-are/?sh=758a7aea6cd5

3. Eduardo Santaella, "What Is Sales Lift," *Mobile Insight*, April 23, 2020, https://mobileinsight.com/what-is-sales-lift/

4. Howard Riell, "Savvy Merchandising and Clever Marketing Can Take Sales Up a Notch," *Produce Business*, November 1, 2019, https://www.producebusiness.com/bananas-are-key-driver-for-produce-department/

CHAPTER 4: TAKE CONTROL OF YOUR DAY

1. Simon Folkard, "Diurnal Variation in Logical Reasoning," *British Journal of Psychology* 66, no. 1 (1975): 1-8, doi: 10.1111/j.2044-8295.1975.tb01433.x

    Timothy H. Monk, Margaret L. Moline, Jeffrey E. Fookson, and Suzanne M. Peetz, "Circadian Determinants of Subjective Alertness," *Journal of Biological Rhythms* 4, no. 4 (1989): 393-404, doi: 10.1177/074873048900400401

    Daniel H. Pink, "The Hidden Pattern of Everyday Life," in *When: The Scientific Secrets of Perfect Timing* (New York: Riverhead Books, 2018), 9-35.

2. Ana Adan, Simon N. Archer, Maria Paz Hidalgo, Lee Di Milia, Vincenzo Natale, and Christoph Randler, "Circadian Typology: A Comprehensive Review," *Chronobiology International* 29, no. 9 (2012): 1153-75, doi: 10.3109/07420528.2012.71997

    Daniel H. Pink, "The Hidden Pattern of Everyday Life," in *When: The Scientific Secrets of Perfect Timing* (New York: Riverhead Books, 2018), 9-35.

    Till Roenneberg, Tim Kuehnle, Myriam Juda, Thomas Kantermann, Karla Allebrandt, Marijke Gordijn, and Martha Merrow, "Epidemiology of the Human Circadian Clock," *Sleep Medicine Reviews* 11, no. 6 (2007): 429-38, doi: 10.1016/j.smrv.2007.07.005

3. Cindi May, "The Inspiration Paradox: Your Best Creative Time Is Not When You Think," *Scientific American*, March 6, 2012, https://www.scientificamerican.com/article/your-best-creative-time-not-when-you-think/

Daniel H. Pink, "The Hidden Pattern of Everyday Life," in *When: The Scientific Secrets of Perfect Timing* (New York: Riverhead Books, 2018), 9-35.

Mareike B. Wieth and Rose T. Zacks, "Time of Day Effects on Problem Solving: When the Non-Optimal Is Optimal," *Thinking & Reasoning* 17, no. 4 (2011): 387-401, doi: 10.1080/13546783.2011.625663

4. Ana Adan, Simon N. Archer, Maria Paz Hidalgo, Lee Di Milia, Vincenzo Natale, and Christoph Randler, "Circadian Typology: A Comprehensive Review," *Chronobiology International* 29, no. 9 (2012): 1153-75, doi: 10.3109/07420528.2012.71997

Daniel H. Pink, "The Hidden Pattern of Everyday Life," in *When: The Scientific Secrets of Perfect Timing* (New York: Riverhead Books, 2018), 9-35.

Franzis Preckel, Anastasiya A. Lipnevick, Sandra Schneider, and Richard D. Roberts, "Chronotype, Cognitive Abilities, and Academic Achievement: A Meta-Analytic Investigation," *Learning and Individual Differences* 21, no. 5 (2011): 483–92, doi: 10.1016/j.lindif.2011.07.003

Till Roenneberg, Anna Wirz-Justice, and Martha Merrow, "Life Between Clocks: Daily Temporal Patterns of Human Chronotypes," *Journal of Biological Rhythms* 18, no. 1 (2003): 80–90.

Jacques Taillard, Pierre Philip, Jean-François Chastang, and Bernard Bioulac, "Validation of Horne and Ostberg Morningness-Eveningness Questionnaire in a Middle-Aged Population of French Workers," *Journal of Biological Rhythms* 19, no 1 (2004): 76-86, doi: 10.1177/0748730403259849

5. Simon Folkard, "Diurnal Variation in Logical Reasoning," *British Journal of Psychology* 66, no. 1 (1975): 1-8, doi: 10.1111/j.2044-8295.1975.tb01433.x

Sooyeol Kim, Seonghee Cho, and YoungAh Park, "Daily Microbreaks in a Self-Regulatory Resources Lens: Perceived Health Climate as a Contextual Moderator via Microbreak Autonomy," *Journal of Applied Psychology* 107, no. 1 (2022): 60-77, doi: 10.1037/apl0000891

Timothy H. Monk, Margaret L. Moline, Jeffrey E. Fookson, and Suzanne M. Peetz, "Circadian Determinants of Subjective

Alertness," *Journal of Biological Rhythms* 4, no. 4 (1989): 393-404, doi: 10.1177/074873048900400401

Daniel H. Pink, "Afternoons and Coffee Spoons: The Power of Breaks, and the Promise of Lunch, and the Case of a Modern Siesta," in *When: The Scientific Secrets of Perfect Timing* (New York: Riverhead Books, 2018), 49-83.

Hans Henrick Sievertsen, Francesca Gino, and Marco Piovesan, "Cognitive Fatigue Influences Students' Performance on Standardized Tests," *Proceedings of the Natural Academy of Sciences* 113, no. 10 (2016): 2621-24, doi: 10.1073/pnas.1516947113

6. Jo Barton and Jules Pretty, "What Is the Best Dose of Nature and Green Exercise for Improving Mental Health? A Multi-Study Analysis," *Environmental Science & Technology* 44, no. 10 (2010): 3947-55, doi: 10.1021/es903183r

Audrey Bergouignan, Kristina T. Legget, Nathan De Jong, Elizabeth Kealy, Janet Nikolovski, Jack L. Groppel, Chris Jordan, Raphaela O'Day, James O. Hill, and Daniel H. Bessesen, "Effects of Frequent Interruptions of Prolonged Sitting on Self-Perceived Levels of Energy, Mood, Food Cravings and Cognitive Function," *International Journal of Behavioral Nutrition and Physical Activity* 13, no. 1 (2016): 13-24, doi: 10.11.86/s12966-016-0437-z

Kristen M. Finkbeiner, Paul N. Russell, and William S. Helton, "Rest Improves Performance, Nature Improves Happiness: Assessment of Break Periods on the Abbreviated Vigilance Task," *Consciousness and Cognition* 42 (2016): 277-85, doi: 10.1016/j.concog.2016.04.005

Sooyeol Kim, YoungAh Park, and Lucille Headrick, "Daily Microbreaks and Job Performance: General Work Engagement as a Cross-Level Moderator," *Journal of Applied Psychology* 103, no. 7 (2018): 772-86, doi: 10.1037/apl0000308

Sooyeol Kim, Young AhPark, and Qikon Niu, "Micro-Break Activities at Work to Recover from Daily Work Demands," *Journal of Organizational Behavior* 38, no. 1 (2017): 28-41, doi: 10.1002/job.2019

Elizabeth K. Nisbet and John M. Zelenski, "Understanding Nearby Nature: Affective Forecasting Errors Obscure the Happy Path to Sustainability," *Psychological Science* 22, no. 9 (2011): 1101-6, doi: 10.1177/0956797611418527

Marily Oppezzo and Daniel Schwartz, "Give Your Ideas Some Legs: The Positive Effect on Walking on Creative Thinking," *Journal of Experimental Psychology: Learning, Memory, and Cognition* 40, no. 4 (2014): 114-52, doi: 10.1037/a0036577

Daniel H. Pink, "Afternoons and Coffee Spoons: The Power of Breaks, and the Promise of Lunch, and the Case of a Modern Siesta," in *When: The Scientific Secrets of Perfect Timing* (New York: Riverhead Books, 2018), 49-83.

Johannes Wendsche, Winfried Hacker, Jürgen Wegge, Nadine Schrod, Katharina Roitzsch, and Anne Tomaschek, "Rest Break Organization in Geriatric Care and Turnover. A Multimethod Cross-Sectional Study," *International Journal of Nursing Studies* 51, no. 9 (2014): 1246-57, doi: 10.1016/j.ijnurstu.2014.01.006

Li-Ling Wu, Kuo-Ming Wang, Po-I Liao, and Yi-Ching Huang, "Effects of an 8-Week Outdoor Brisk Walking Program on Fatigue in Hi-Tech Industry Employees: A Randomized Control Trial," *Workplace Health & Safety* 63, no. 10 (2015): 436-45, doi: 10.1177/2165079915589685

7. Sooyeol Kim, Young AhPark, and Qikon Niu, "Micro-Break Activities at Work to Recover from Daily Work Demands," *Journal of Organizational Behavior* 38, no. 1 (2016): 28-41.

Daniel H. Pink, "Afternoons and Coffee Spoons: The Power of Breaks, and the Promise of Lunch, and the Case of a Modern Siesta," in *When: The Scientific Secrets of Perfect Timing* (New York: Riverhead Books, 2018), 49-83.

Marjaana Sianoja, Ulla Kinnunen, Jessica de Bloom, Kalevi Korpela, and Sabine Geurts, "Recovery During Lunch Breaks: Testing Long-Term Relations with Energy Levels at Work," *Scandinavian Journal of Work and Organizational Psychology* 1, no. 1 (2016): 1-12, doi: 10.16993/sjwop.13

CHAPTER 5: HELP YOUR TEAM SUCCEED

1. Eric Schmidt, Jonathan Rosenberg, and Alan Eagle, "Team First," in *Trillion Dollar Coach: The Leadership Playbook of Silicon Valley's Bill Campbell* (New York: HarperCollins, 2019), 107-53.

2. Wayne Baker, Rob Cross, and Melissa Wooten, "Positive Organizational Network Analysis and Energizing Relationships," in *Positive Organizational Scholarship*, ed. Kim S. Cameron, Jane E. Dutton, and Robert E. Quinn (San Francisco: Berrett-Koehler, 2003), 328-42.

Kim Cameron, *Positive Leadership: Strategies for Extraordinary Performance*, 2nd ed. (Oakland, CA: Berrett-Koehler), 2012.

Rob Cross, Wayne Baker, and Andrew Parker, "What Creates Energy in Organizations?," *Sloan Management Review* 44, no. 4 (2003): 51-56.

Anne-Kathrin Kleine, Cort W. Rudolph, and Hannes Zacher, "Thriving at Work: A Meta-Analysis," *Journal of Organizational Behavior* 40 (2019): 973-99, doi: 10.1002/job.2375

3. Kyle Benson, "The Magic Relationship Ratio, According to Science," *The Gottman Institute: A Research-Based Approach to Relationships,* https://www.gottman.com/blog/the-magic-relationship-ratio-according-science/

4. Kyle Benson, "The Magic Relationship Ratio, According to Science," *The Gottman Institute: A Research-Based Approach to Relationships,* https://www.gottman.com/blog/the-magic-relationship-ratio-according-science/

5. Marcial Losada and Emily Heaphy, "The Role of Positivity and Connectivity in the Performance of Business Teams," *American Behavioral Scientist* 47, no. 6 (February 2004): 740-65, doi: 10.1177/0002764203260208

6. John Paul Stephens, Emily D. Heaphy, Abraham Carmeli, Gretchen M. Spreitzer, and Jane E. Dutton, "Relationship Quality of Virtuousness: Emotional Carrying Capacity as a Source of Individual and Team Resilience," *Journal of Applied Behavioral Science* 49, no. 1 (2013): 13-41, doi: 10.1177/0021886312471193

7. John Paul Stephens, Emily D. Heaphy, Abraham Carmeli, Gretchen M. Spreitzer, and Jane E. Dutton, "Relationship Quality of Virtuousness: Emotional Carrying Capacity as a Source of Individual and Team Resilience," *Journal of Applied Behavioral Science* 49, no. 1 (2013): 13-41, doi: 10.1177/0021886312471193

Sooyeol Kim, YoungAh Park, and Lucille Headrick, "Daily Microbreaks and Job Performance: General Work Engagement as a Cross-Level Moderator," *Journal of Applied Psychology* 103, no. 7 (2018): 772-86, doi: 10.1037/ap10000308

8. Rendelle Bolton, Caroline Logan, and Jody Hoffer Gittell, "Revisiting Relational Coordination: A Systematic Review," *Journal of Applied Behavioral Science* (February 15, 2021): 1-33, doi: 10.1177/0021886321991597

Mark D. Cannon and Amy C. Edmondson, "Failing to Learn and Learning to Fail (Intelligently): How Great Organizations Put Failure to Work to Innovate and Improve," *Long Range Planning* 38 (2005): 299-319, doi: 10.1016/j.lrp.2005.04.005

Abraham Carmeli and Jody Hoffer Gittell, "High-Quality Relationships, Psychological Safety, and Learning from Failures in Work Organizations," *Journal of Organizational Behavior* 30 (2009): 709-29, doi: 10.1002/job.565

Amy Edmondson, "Psychological Safety and Learning Behavior in Work Teams," *Administrative Science Quarterly* 44 (1999): 350-83, doi: 10.2307/2666999

Reuven Hirak, Ann Chunyan Peng, Abraham Carmeli, and John M. Schaubroeck, "Linking Leader Inclusiveness to Work Unit Performance: The Importance of Psychological Safety and Learning from Failures," *Leadership Quarterly* 23 (2012): 107-17, doi: 10.1016/j.leaqua.2011.11.009

John Schaubroeck, Abraham Carmeli, Sarena Bhatia, and Etty Paz, "Enabling Team Learning When Members Are Prone to Contentious Communication: The Role of Team Leader Coaching," *Human Relations* 69, no. 8 (2016): 1709-27, doi: 10.1177/0018726715622673

Manuel Stühlinger, Jan B. Schumutz, and Gudela Grote, "I Hear You, but Do I Understand? The Relationship of a Shared Professional Language With Quality of Care and Job Satisfaction," *Frontiers in Psychology*, (June 4, 2019), Article 1310, doi: 10.3389/fpsyg.2019.01310

9. Mark D. Cannon and Amy C. Edmondson, "Failing to Learn and Learning to Fail (Intelligently): How Great Organizations Put Failure to Work to Innovate and Improve," *Long Range Planning* 38 (2005): 299-319, doi: 10.1016/j.lrp.2005.04.005

10. Abraham Carmeli and Judy Hoffer Gittell, "High-Quality Relationships, Psychological Safety, and Learning from Failures in Work Organizations," *Journal of Organizational Behavior* 30 (2009): 709-29, doi: 10.1002/job.565

Amy Edmondson, "Psychological Safety and Learning Behavior in Work Teams," *Administrative Science Quarterly* 44 (1999): 350-83, doi: 10.2307/2666999

Reuven Hirak, Ann Chunyan Peng, Abraham Carmeli, and John M. Schaubroeck, "Linking Leader Inclusiveness to Work Unit Performance: The Importance of Psychological Safety and Learning from Failures," *Leadership Quarterly* 23 (2012): 107-17, doi: 10.1016/j.leaqua.2011.11.009

11. Rendelle Bolton, Caroline Logan, and Jody Hoffer Gittell, "Revisiting Relational Coordination: A Systematic Review," *Journal of Applied Behavioral Science* (February 15, 2021): 1-33, doi: 10.1177/0021886321991597

Amy Edmondson, "Psychological Safety and Learning Behavior in Work Teams," *Administrative Science Quarterly* 44 (1999): 350-83, doi: 10.2307/2666999

Reuven Hirak, Ann Chunyan Peng, Abraham Carmeli, and John M. Schaubroeck, "Linking Leader Inclusiveness to Work Unit Performance: The Importance of Psychological Safety and Learning from Failures," *Leadership Quarterly* 23 (2012): 107-17, doi: 10.1016/j.leaqua.2011.11.009

John Schaubroeck, Abraham Carmeli, Sarena Bhatia, and Etty Paz, "Enabling Team Learning When Members Are Prone to Contentious Communication: The Role of Team Leader Coaching," *Human Relations* 69, no. 8 (2016): 1709-27, doi: 10.1177/0018726715622673

12. Mark D. Cannon and Amy C. Edmondson, "Failing to Learn and Learning to Fail (Intelligently): How Great Organizations Put Failure to Work to Innovate and Improve," *Long Range Planning* 38 (2005): 299-319, doi: 10.1016/j.lrp.2005.04.005

CHAPTER 6: CREATE BEST PRACTICES

1. Daniel H. Pink, "Clarify: Making Your Message Count," *Masterclass* lecture, 2021, https://www.masterclass.com/

CHAPTER 8: GET THE YES

1. Daniel H. Pink, "Beginnings, Middles, and Endings," *Masterclass* lecture, 2021, https://www.masterclass.com/

2. Daniel H. Pink, "Beginnings, Middles, and Endings," *Masterclass* lecture, 2021, https://www.masterclass.com/

3. Daniel H. Pink, "Create a Connection by Mimicking," *Masterclass* lecture, 2021, https://www.masterclass.com/

4. Chris Voss, "Bending Reality," *Masterclass* lecture, 2021, https://www.masterclass.com/

5. Chris Voss, "Tactical Empathy," *Masterclass* lecture, 2021, https://www.masterclass.com/

6. Adam Tobin and Dan Klein, "How to Master Impromptu Communication: Speaking Without a Net," Podcast by Matt Abrahams, *Think Fast Talk Smart: Communication Techniques,* January 15, 2020, https://www.gsb.stanford.edu/business-podcasts/think-fast-talk-smart-podcast

7. Vanessa Van Edwards, *Captivate: The Science of Succeeding with People* (New York: Portfolio/Penguin, 2017).

CHAPTER 9: PRESENT LIKE A PRO

1. Chris Anderson, "How to Give a Killer Presentation," *Harvard Business Review,* June 2013, https://hbr.org/2013/06/how-to-give-a-killer-presentation

2. Chris Anderson, "How to Give a Killer Presentation," *Harvard Business Review,* June 2013, https://hbr.org/2013/06/how-to-give-a-killer-presentation

3. Sims Wyeth, "Do You Read from a Script? Should You?," *Presentation Guru,* April 20, 2017, https://www.presentation-guru.com/do-you-read-from-a-script-should-you/

4. Sims Wyeth, "Do You Read from a Script? Should You?," *Presentation Guru,* April 20, 2017, https://www.presentation-guru.com/do-you-read-from-a-script-should-you/

5. Sims Wyeth, "Do You Read from a Script? Should You?," *Presentation Guru,* April 20, 2017, https://www.presentation-guru.com/do-you-read-from-a-script-should-you/

6. Adam Tobin and Dan Klein, "How to Master Impromptu Communication: Speaking Without a Net," Podcast by Matt Abrahams, *Think Fast Talk Smart: Communication Techniques,* January 15, 2020, https://www.gsb.stanford.edu/business-podcasts/think-fast-talk-smart-podcast

7. Adam Tobin and Dan Klein, "How to Master Impromptu Communication: Speaking Without a Net," Podcast by Matt Abrahams, *Think Fast Talk Smart: Communication Techniques,* January 15, 2020, https://www.gsb.stanford.edu/business-podcasts/think-fast-talk-smart-podcast

8. Janet Zaretsky, "5 Powerful Tips From the Best TED Talks to Improve Your Public Speaking Skills," *Janet Zaretsky,* December 11, 2019, https://janetzaretsky.com/best-ted-talks-tips-public-speaking-coaching/

9. Sims Wyeth, "Do You Read from a Script? Should You?," *Presentation Guru,* April 20, 2017, https://www.presentation-guru.com/do-you-read-from-a-script-should-you/

10. Adam Tobin and Dan Klein, "How to Master Impromptu Communication: Speaking Without a Net," Podcast by Matt

Abrahams, *Think Fast Talk Smart: Communication Techniques*, January 15, 2020, https://www.gsb.stanford.edu/business-podcasts/think-fast-talk-smart-podcast

11. Jesse Freeman, "The Anatomy of an Amazon 6-Pager," *The Writing Cooperative*, July 16, 2020, https://writingcooperative.com/the-anatomy-of-an-amazon-6-pager-fc79f31a41c9

CHAPTER 10: INVEST IN YOUR FUTURE

1. Stephanie L. Brown, Randolph M. Nesse, Amiram D. Vinokur, and Dylan M. Smith, "Providing Social Support May Be More Beneficial Than Receiving It: Results from a Prospective Study on Mortality," *Psychological Science* 14, no. 4 (2003): 320-27, doi: 10.1111/1467-9280.14461

   Kim Cameron, "Positive Relationships," in *Positive Leadership: Strategies for Extraordinary Performance*, 2nd ed. (Oakland, CA: Berrett-Koehler, 2012), 45-83.

2. Zahra Amjad, Sami Ullah Pirzada Sabri, Muhammad Ilyas, and Afshaan Hameed, "Informal Relationships at Workplace and Employee Performance: A Study of Employees Private Higher Education Sector," *Pakistan Journal of Commerce and Social Sciences* 9, no. 1 (2015): 303-21.

   Jessica R. Methot, Jeffrey A. Lepine, Nathan P. Podsakoff, and Jessica Siegel Christian, "Are Workplace Friendships a Mixed Blessing? Exploring Tradeoffs of Multiplex Relationships and Their Associations with Job Performance," *Personnel Psychology* 69 (2016): 311-55, doi: 10.111/peps.12109

3. Zahra Amjad, Sami Ullah Pirzada Sabri, Muhammad Ilyas, and Afshaan Hameed, "Informal Relationships at Workplace and Employee Performance: A Study of Employees Private Higher Education Sector," *Pakistan Journal of Commerce and Social Sciences* 9, no. 1 (2015): 303-21.

   Jessica R. Methot, Jeffrey A. Lepine, Nathan P. Podsakoff, and Jessica Siegel Christian, "Are Workplace Friendships a Mixed Blessing? Exploring Tradeoffs of Multiplex Relationships and Their Associations with Job Performance," *Personnel Psychology* 69 (2016): 311-55, doi: 10.111/peps.12109

ABOUT THE AUTHORS

Randy Ornstein has 22 years of experience in the Beverage industry, working in leadership roles at both Anheuser-Busch InBev and Gopuff. He completed his BA in Business Marketing at Indiana University and his Walton Executive MBA at the University of Arkansas.

Hayley Ornstein received her PhD in Counseling Psychology from the University of Oklahoma. Her professional experience includes therapy, evaluation, and teaching.